IS THE _ _ _ _ _ _ _ _ _ _ _

POPE PAUL VI INVALID?

ಓ ಐ

Is the New Mass of Pope Paul VI Invalid?

IS THE NEW MASS OF POPE PAUL VI INVALID?

A Response to the Arguments Against its Validity and Legality

A Preliminary Study

By

Adam S. Miller

Tower of David Publications

Is the New Mass of Pope Paul VI Invalid?

Tower of David Publications
A division of Tower of David Ministry
11910 Wonder Ct.
Monrovia, MD 21770

E-mail: tower_of_david@netscape.com
www.towerofdavid.com

Cover design by Christopher Morsey

Printed in the United States of America
Lulu Enterprizes
www.lulu.com

ISBN 978-1-4116-9978-6

CONTENTS

If anyone says that the ceremonies, vestments, and outward signs, which the Catholic Church uses in the celebration of Masses, are incentives to impiety rather than the services of piety: let him be anathema. (Council of Trent, Canon 7, On the Holy Sacrifice of the Mass, Denz. 954)

INTRODUCTION

There is a grave crisis in the Church today. For laity and clergy alike, it is a crisis of, faith, of morals, of authority, of praxis, and of liturgical life. If confusion is produced by this crisis, it is made worse when doubt is cast on matters that should never be questioned by the faithful. This is the case when the validity and legality of the sacraments, the life giving channels of God's saving and sanctifying grace to men, are questioned. Because of questions raised against it, doubts exist among some traditionalists as to the validity of the Rite of Mass promulgated by Pope Paul VI in 1969. The present work is concerned with these questions. It is undertaken in the surety that anyone who does not accept the validity of the sacraments in their present form is excommunicated from the Church of the Faithful, outside of which there is no salvation. Such was declared by then Prefect of the Congregation for the Doctrine of the Faith, Cardinal Ratzinger (cf. *Ad Tuendam Fidem* published with the note of the CDF in the *Acta Apostolicae sedis* 90 [6/30/1998] 542-551).

To be sure, it is sometimes alleged on grounds of moral theology, that Catholics with any doubt about the validity of a particular sacrament cannot in good conscience participate in it. However, such works of moral theology which address this matter are dealing only with the occasion of when an individual priest or some group makes changes to the sacramental form of the particular rite being used, and not to that which has been promulgated and approved for universal use by the Roman Pontiff himself, as is the case with the Mass of Pope Paul VI. (We address this point in Part VI.) In truth, as laymen we have no business "doubting" anything in regard to the Sacred Mysteries of the Sacraments. Thus, when the Church promulgates and pronounces a particular sacramental rite to be a sufficient and proper vehicle for conferring a particular sacrament, not simply is it valid and are the faithful obliged to accept it as such, but no layman has a moral right (let alone duty) to cause others to doubt because of his own subjective mental state of doubt. Besides being proud and impertinent, it is scandalous to call into question the validity of sacraments approved by the Church and to cause others to do the same.

1

The purpose of the present work is to examine, critique, and refute questions (and conclusions) that have cast doubt on the validity and legality of the Novus Ordo Missae: New Order of Mass (N.O.M. for short) promulgated by Pope Paul VI. This work should be approached more as a study than as simply reading material, for to benefit fully the reader must be studiously attentive to the arguments herein.

What this work is NOT:

• not a critique of the entire N.O.M. in general. In other words, this is not a critique of the ceremonies surrounding it which contribute to a loss of the sense of the sacred; not a critique of the offertory prayers, which have deleted nearly all references to propitiatory sacrifice; not a critique of the other prayers (Propers, etc.) which omit much Catholic theology/teaching;

  • not an examination of the abuses that occur in many N.O. Masses;

  • not a defense of the N.O.M. in preference over the traditional Latin/Roman Rite;

What this work is:

• A critical and detailed examination of the critiques of the new sacramental form of the N.O.M. offered by Patrick Henry Omlor and others;

  • A refutation of the arguments denying the validity of the N.O.M.;
  • A refutation of the arguments denying the legality of the N.O.M.;
  • A defense only of the fact that the N.O.M. can be said validly, even with the use of the words "for all" in the Consecration of the wine.

Patrick Henry Omlor: *The Robber Church*:

The Robber Church (Ontario, Canada; Silvio Mattachione & Co., 1998) is a compilation of the works of Patrick Henry Omlor. Mr. Omlor has presented a substantial amount of arguments and documentation to buttress his position, putting forth the position that the validity of the N.O.M., particularly in its various vernacular translations, is at best highly doubtful, at worst it is null and void, and thus invalid. The more significant works pertinent to the validity or invalidity of the N.O.M. within this compilation are:

- "Questioning The Validity of the Masses Using the New, All-English Canon" (pp. 13-81);
- "Interdum" (eight issues: 91- 215)
- "Questioning the Validity of McCarthy's Case" (233-266) and "Excerpts from Monsignor McCarthy Again!" (323-330);
- "The Necessary Signification in the Sacramental Form of the Holy Eucharist" (267-322)
- "The Charlatans" (331-344);
- "No Mystery of Faith: No Mass" (354-374)
- "Denotes Does Not Imply Accomplishes" (375-376)

Many ill-informed and/or radical traditionalist Catholics have been influenced by and use his arguments to cause others to doubt the validity of the N.O.M. I will state now, in summary form, Patrick H. Omlor's Position: Mr. Omlor states that IF the new form "involves an essential change in meaning," and he believes that it does, THEN "the sacrament has clearly been rendered invalid" (page 28, #35). He claims that he shall prove this to be the case, and will use St. Thomas Aquinas as his authority. Mr. Omlor holds that the new "sacramental form," particularly in the all-English translation of the new Canon, signifies an essential change in meaning (p.28), and that it suppresses what is essential and signifies falsely (pp. 39ff); hence "invalidity through defect of form" (see p. 218-219: "Our Case in the briefest Terms").

Defect of form is defined as a change in signification, a change in the essential meaning of the words. Omlor argues that the change of "for many" into "for all" in the new consecration formula is a change that does not signify the same reality (nor the same theology) as do the words "for many." According to Mr. Omlor and others, the words "FOR ALL":

1. fail to convey the sense of efficacy (i.e. the effective application of Christ's shed blood upon many, but not all men), and denote only the sense of sufficiency (i.e. that Christ simply died for all men, with no reference to the actual application of His Precious Blood to believers), even though the

constant teaching of the Church is that the Holy Sacrifice of the Mass is the *efficacious* application of the graces and merits of Christ's shed Blood. Thus the new form, "… is to be shed for you and for all so that sins may be forgiven," destroys the true sense of the proper form (pp. 31-34);

2. if not conveying the sense of sufficiency, but still referring to the efficacy of the Sacrifice, then the heresy of universal salvation is signified, thus invalidating the new rite (i.e. Christ's shed blood is effectively applied to ALL men, thus all men will be saved - which is contrary to Divine Revelation and Church dogma);

3. signify all men of all time, not the Elect, or the members of the Mystical Body of Christ, or those upon whom the shed blood is efficacious. This means that the new form confuses, if not denies, the effect of the Sacrament as not signifying the union of the Mystical Body (the reality or effect of the Sacrament). Thus the words "for you and for all (men)" not only fail to convey this essential signification of the Mystical Body, but on the contrary, they signify falsely! (pp. 39-42)

This means, according to Mr. Omlor and others, that the substance of the sacrament has been changed, for there is a "defect in form," hence the invalidity of the N.O.M. (The "substance" of a sacrament involves two realities: 1: that which makes it what it is, and without which the Sacrament would not be and, 2: those things which Christ the Lord Himself prescribed must be maintained in the sacramental signs.) Mr. Omlor states that his concern is with the substitution of the form: "for you and for many unto the remission of sins" with "for you and for all so that sins may be forgiven" (p.29). Later on, Mr. Omlor admits that: "EVERYTHING is at stake on THIS point" (p. 222; capitals are my addition). Taking Mr. Omlor at his word, this is what we shall concentrate upon. The burden of proof, to determine that the new consecration formula of the wine does in fact signify an essential change in meaning, is upon Mr. Omlor.

Another point to be mentioned is that Mr. Omlor admits that his position concerning the short form of the Consecration as being insufficient for validity is only an opinion, and even then that his opinion is only probable. He also recognizes (p. 355, # 5) that the matter concerning whether the short form ("This is the chalice of my Blood") or the long form (entire consecration form) suffices for validity has not been decided definitively by the Church. Thus, Mr. Omlor can only offer an opinion on this point, though it is one that has some historical backing. (See St. Thomas Aquinas, *Summa Theologica*, III, Q.78, Art.3)

The crux of Mr. Omlor's argument against the short form as being sufficient for validity is that, according to Pope Leo XIII's Bull, *Apostolicae Curae* (1896), "all know that the Sacraments of the New Law, as sensible and efficient signs of invisible grace, must both signify the grace which they effect, and effect the grace which they signify... The form consequently cannot be apt or sufficient for a Sacrament which omits what it must essentially signify." According to Mr. Omlor, the short form of the Consecration fails to signify in an unambiguous manner the remission of the sins of the members of Christ's Mystical Body, and also fails to signify the union thereof.

The point also could be made that the words "for many" nor "for All" do not affect the consecration which preceded these words because they have no effect upon the signification of THIS IS MY BODY, THIS IS MY BLOOD. It is these words which signify the change and the reality: logic and grammar demand it, and theology can never contradict right reason, Vatican I defined this *De Fide Definita*. However, we will not be arguing for the short form opinion against the long form opinion, which is Mr. Omlor's position. For the sake of argument on this point, we will argue with Mr. Omlor (and others) in his own court and presume as fact that the short form alone is not sufficient to signify the proper effect and thus confect the Sacrament.

I offer as my Points of Refutation the following:

1. Point I: Signification is in fact not changed with the use of "for all," nor does it signify falsely, for the meaning of the words do not necessitate such, hence the essence of the sacramental form is not affected, but kept intact;

2. Point II: The principle of supplying a Catholic understanding refutes the anti-"for all" position, and proves that "for all" in fact provides proper signification, for there is nothing prohibiting the new form from meaning such;

3. Point III: The principle of logical necessity is lacking in the anti-valid/doubtful validity position; without this necessity, the anti-valid/doubtful validity position cannot be sustained;

4. Point IV: Papal authority in regards to *Quo Primum*, and its use in the legislation of N.O.M. as a valid rite, is both protected by the indefectibility of the Church and is validly exercised;

It might be asked: Why do I, a traditional Catholic apologist and educator, take the side of defending the validity and legality of the N.O.M., despite the fact that it is a clear break from tradition? I do so for three reasons: 1) because Catholics are not allowed to deny any truth, natural or supernatural, but are obligated to recognize the truth where it is found and defend it if need be; 2) because the same authority (papal) which approved all the traditional rites also approved and promulgated the new rite of Mass; and 3) because Mr. Omlor welcomes corrections.

Mr. Omlor admits that his arguments are not "beyond question or challenge," and that "[w]hen more weighty arguments (either for or against [his]) are advanced, [he] will welcome them." Mr. Omlor goes on to quote St. Anselm, adopting the saint's attitude: "If there is anything that calls for correction I do not refuse the correction" (see Preface to "Questioning the Validity;" also found on p. 22 in *The Robber Church*). This is what I have set out to accomplish.

Every work this author has read which argues against the validity of the NO Mass, or even argues that a serious doubt exists, fail to recognize the first three points just listed above. So it appears that Mr. Omlor has not encountered the arguments of this author. One fatal fact of Mr. Omlor's, as well as others who hold his position, is that they all presume that the words "for all" necessarily mean "all men of all time," and can not have any other meaning. We will demonstrate that this is in fact not the case. (Each section has prominent objections answered.)

POINT I:

'ALL' vs 'MANY'

There are many who hold that with the use of the words "for all" instead of "for many" in the Consecration of the wine the N.O.M. is (or may be) rendered invalid. Is this true? In order for the I.C.E.L. (International Commission on English in the Liturgy) mistranslation of *pro-multis* ("for many") as "for all" to succeed in making the New Mass consecration invalid it must NECESSARILY involve a change in the over-all meaning as well as necessarily change the signification. This is the very condition presumed by Pope St. Pius V in the Decree, *De Defectibus*, which would bring into effect his solemn declaration. The sainted pontiff states:

> "If anyone removes or changes anything in the Form of the Consecration of the Body and Blood, *and by this change of words does not signify the same thing as these words do*, he does not confect the sacrament." (italics added)

Saint Thomas Aquinas gave witness to this same point when he wrote that:

> "Words belong to a sacramental form by reason of the SENSE SIGNIFIED by them. Consequently, any addition or suppression of words which do not add to, nor take away from, the ESSENTIAL SENSE does NOT destroy the essence of the Sacrament." (*Summa Theologica* III, q.60, art.8)

It is clear from this historic teaching that it is not strictly the changing of words which invalidates or fails to confect the sacrament, but where BY such a change of words the same thing or the same sense is not signified. It will be demonstrated that the sense signified by the new sacramental form in the N.O.M. does not take away from the same and essential sense of the traditional form. Patrick H. Omlor, and certain other radical traditionalists, presumes that "for all" necessitates a change in signification; that these words change the essential sense. It is incumbent upon Mr. Omlor, et al, to prove that the new form in fact does not signify the same thing as the traditional form.

It should also be noted that this restriction in *De Defectibus* is primarily meant to stop individuals, particularly priests in the celebration of Mass, from changing anything in the form according to THAT particular Rite. It does not address the matter of the different sacramental forms between rites. In fact, hardly ANY of the other traditional Catholic Rites (i.e. Eastern Rites) have the exact same Consecration form, yet all are valid (See Appendix I). This fact is what is more relevant to our topic, and not the restrictions or changes within any particular Rite, which is what *De Defectibus* was addressing.

This work will examine the fact that the change of "for many" into "for all" is NOT a change that signifies something different from what these words ("for many") do. This is the key qualification and condition of *De Defectibus*; and the new form in the N.O.M. does not fall under this solemn prohibition. This work will demonstrate that the essential signification is not changed in the new form, particularly when understood in light of Catholic teaching; and this is how numerous prayers from ALL the rites must be approached and understood. Before we do this, a few important points must be made concerning the Holy Mass.

First: we must define the word "valid." What is meant by "valid" in sacramental theology?

valid: producing the desired effect or results; effective in accomplishing its purpose (cf. Pohle-Preuss, *The Sacraments*, Dogmatic Theology series, vol. VIII).

At a valid Mass, the bread and wine change into the Body and Blood of Christ at the Consecration, and at an invalid Mass no such miraculous change occurs. The question of validity is a most important one, since we can never knowingly participate in the worship of an invalid Mass. To do so is to worship mere bread and wine rather than the Incarnate Word –God in the flesh- and this is idolatry, contrary to the 1st Commandment. It follows, then, that participation in an invalid Mass can never fulfill a Catholic's Sunday obligation, nor does such glorify God.

Second: Does the new Mass fail to achieve the desired effect? What are the desired effects of the Holy Sacrifice of the Mass? They are;

-Transubstantiation (the miraculous changing of the bread and wine into the real Body and   Blood of our Lord Jesus Christ);
-The efficacious application of the merits and graces of Christ's Passion to men (thus   propitiation for sins; increase in sanctification);
-The union of the individual with the Mystical Body of Christ;
-Thus, the adoration of God;

Traditionally, the Holy Sacrifice of the Mass is understood as the efficacious application of the graces and merits Christ gained by His death on the cross. This necessarily means, as Trent dogmatically defined, that:

> "although Christ died for all men, all men do not receive the benefit of his death, but only those to whom the merit of His Passion is communicated." (On Justification, chap. 3: Denz. 795)

The argument against the N.O.M. in the vast majority of its translations (which use "for all" instead of "for many") is that the words "for all" necessarily signify that all men in fact do receive the benefit of Christ's death, that is all receive the effective application of His shed blood. It appears that this would signify the heresy of universal salvation – that all men are, or will be, saved and reach Heaven. This is what Patrick Omlor, Father James Wathen, O.S.J. (*The Great Sacrilege*, TAN Books, 1971), Dr. Rama P. Coomaraswamy(*The Problems with the New Mass*, TAN Books, 1990), Fr. Paul Trinchard (*New Mass in Light of the Old*, Marian Pub., 1995), and others, who argue either against the validity of the N.O.M. or seriously doubt it, hold that the words "for all" signify. The works of these and other men include comments on the over-all tone and spirit of the new Mass and its surrounding prayers. But we are not dealing with these since these deficiencies of the other prayers of the new Mass have neither a direct or intrinsic effect upon whether or not the consecration prayers of the new Rite confect the sacrament.

The aforementioned authors bring up arguments against the use of "for all" as having historic precedent. The Roman Catechism, also known as the Catechism of the Council of Trent, states:

> With reason, therefore, were the words, 'for all' not used, as in this place [in the Mass] the fruits of the Passion are alone spoken of, and, to the elect only did that bring the fruit of salvation. (Part II, Chapter IV, Question 24)

Let us look directly at the matter of the words "for all." Does this term signify, and necessarily so, all men of all time? No. By the dictates of logic, the words "for all" do not necessarily mean for all men of all time. "For all" can be understood in an orthodox manner as meaning for all of the elect, or for all upon whom the shed Blood of Christ is efficacious. Therefore, "for all" does not necessitate an unorthodox meaning, or a meaning contrary to Sacred Tradition concerning the end and efficacy of the Sacrifice of the Mass. Those who argue that "for all" invalidates the New Mass depend upon "for all" as NECESSARILY signifying that which is contrary to orthodox Catholic teaching concerning the Mass. In other words, those who argue against validity hold that "for all" MUST of necessity signify something other than all of the Elect, or for all upon whom the shed Blood of Christ is efficacious. But they do NOT have this necessity. Hence the failure of their arguments and the invalidity of their position. (This point will be developed further in "Point III" below.)

We should be clear by what is meant by "signification." It refers to that reality which the words signify. The notion or concept of signification refers to the three distinct realities in the Holy Sacrifice of the Mass listed previously:

1. Signification of the miraculous change: Transubstantiation;

2. Signification of the efficacious application of the merits/graces of the Holy Sacrifice, viz., Sanctifying grace, the strengthening of the soul, etc.

10

3. Signification of the effect (or reality) of the Sacrament, viz., union with the Mystical Body of Christ.

These are all part of the desired result or effect of the Mass. The laws of logic and grammar make clear that neither the words "for many" or "for all" have a role in denoting or signifying Transubstantiation (point 1). Thus, one could argue that Transubstantiation has already occurred by the time the words "for many/for all" are pronounced. However, as noted before, this work will NOT argue along these lines since one can also argue that to denote does not necessarily imply an accomplished effect or result. (This is precisely the position of Mr. Omlor and others on this point.)

Now, those who deny or at least doubt the validity of the new Sacramental form will ask the following concerning # 2: Since the Mass is the efficacious application of the grace Christ gained by His death on the cross, does not the mistranslation of *pro multis* as "for all" necessitate a change in signification from orthodox Catholic theology concerning the efficacious nature of the Holy Sacrifice of the Mass? Isn't this so, especially since all men do NOT receive the benefit of his death, thus, not all men are saved? Asked another way: Do the words "for all" necessarily teach or signify that what is being stated:

A. is that the fruits of Our Lord's Passion are applied to ALL men of all time?
B. imply the heresy of Universal salvation (that all men will be saved)?
C. imply that the Mass is not an efficacious Sacrifice but only a memorial of Christ's suffering and death on the cross, and therefore mean that the efficacious fruit of our Lord's Passion are NOT applied to the elect only?

No, to each and every one of these questions. The words "for all" do not necessitate any of these interpretations which are contrary to Catholic teaching in general, and concerning the Sacrifice of the Mass in particular. This is so, not because I say so, but because the words in and of themselves do not necessitate such an interpretation. There is nothing in the words of the new sacramental form which prohibit one from under-standing them with the proper signification, and thus in an orthodox way.

THE USE OF "ALL" AS "MANY" IN SACRED SCRIPTURE

There are, in fact, numerous examples from God's own inspired written Word where "all" does not mean the entirety, or everyone without exception, but rather means "many." If "all" cannot mean "many," and if universality cannot sometimes be qualified as "most of" in Holy Scripture, then Jesus and His Blessed Mother are sinful. For ~

• There is no man who does not sin (III Kings 8:46);
• All of us have gone astray; everyone has turned aside (Isaias 53:6);
• There is not any man who is just. All have turned out of the way. There is not so much as one   who does good; not so much as one! (Rom. 3:10-12; Saint Paul really rubs it in!)
• For ALL have sinned and fall short of the glory of God. (Rom.3:23)

But we know Our Lord and Our Lady were (are) sinless. Thus, "all" does not apply to them, which means its usage is not to be understood as entirely inclusive.

There also are verses where "all" and "many" are used to signify the very same thing. It is declared in Romans, Chapter 5, verse 15, that "by the offense of one, MANY died..." Yet, just a few verses before, with reference to the same truth (i.e. the Fall of Adam and its effects), it is declared that "as sin entered by one man... so death passed upon ALL men" (Rom.5:12; see also 1 Cor.15:22). Here we see "many" and "all" being used interchangeably.

This usage of "all" in Sacred Scripture has always been recognized. St. Jerome, for example, makes this point in his Letter to Pope St. Damasus wherein he states: "'all' is not to be referred to the total sum of things, but to the majority" (Epistle 21, 37). In this letter, the great biblical doctor gives these verses as examples: Luke 15:31, Psalm 13:3, John 10:8, 1 Corinthians 9:22, and Philippians 2:21. St. Jerome also states that this understanding has been "often explained" before. It also has been explained as such since. St. Thomas Aquinas also addressed this issue and stated: "St. Augustine explains 'multi' to mean 'all men,' and this manner of speaking is frequently found in Sacred Scripture" (*Summa Theologica*, Q.75, Reply to Obj. 2).

As a result of these facts from both Sacred Scripture and Tradition, we must conclude that the use of "all" as not meaning the entirety, but many, cannot be an invalid and erroneous use of the term. Nor is it necessarily misleading. We know this for God's own Word uses "all" sometimes to mean not all, but many, and God's Word is infallible and inerrant (unless one wants to posit that Scripture is misleading). Subsequent scholars have always recognized this fact concerning the use of the word "all."

The great scholar, Father Cornelius a Lapide (d.1637), in his masterful work on Sacred Scripture, *The Great Commentary* (1600; trans. Thomas Mossman), makes this very point concerning the word "all." He compares the identical stories found in the Gospels of both Ss. Matthew and Luke concerning Our Lord's cure of St. Peter's mother-in-law. Afterward, "when the sun went down, ALL those who had anyone sick with different diseases brought them to Him; and He, laying hands on EVERY ONE OF THEN, healed them; and devils went out from MANY." Thus says St. Luke (4:40-41). However, St. Matthew has it: "And when evening came, they brought to Him many who were possessed with devils. And He cast out the spirits... and ALL who were sick He healed" (On Matthew 8:16-17).

Here is a clear-cut case of "ALL" meaning MANY and vice-versa! This fact cannot be denied. Therefore, to understand "for all" to mean such can not be considered a word game, nor invalid. God has revealed this usage for us in His written Word.

Even without the biblical examples and testimony from tradition, the laws of both logic and grammar dictate that in and of themselves, the words "for all" do not necessarily contradict orthodox Catholic theology concerning what is happening at this very moment in the Holy Sacrifice of the Mass. The words "for all" can, and when understood in light of Catholic teaching, DO mean: for all upon whom the precious blood is efficacious. Neither the substance nor the essence of the sacramental form is necessarily changed simply by the use of these words. This is also proven by the fact that there is a canon that uses NEITHER "for many" or

13

"for all:" The Anaphora of the ancient Alexandrian Canon (St. Mark's Liturgy) says:

"Take, and all of you drink of it; This is my blood, shed for you, for the remission of sins."

Now, the "you" is in the plural, but it appears that it is in reference only to those whom our Lord is speaking, but we know it cannot be restricted to them. Therefore it requires that the faithful understand it IN LIGHT of Catholic teaching. This also proves that the words "for many" are not absolutely and without question necessary for the confecting of the Sacrament.

What also refutes the position of Mr. Omlor and others is that in the Anaphora of the Apostles from the Chaldean (or East Syrian) Rite in union with Rome (also known as the Rite of Sts. Addai & Maris) the words "for you" are not even present:

"Likewise the cup: He gave thanks and gave it to them and said: This is the Blood of the New Testament which is shed for many for the remission of sins."

This is an approved sacramental form whose validity has never been questioned, yet it does not contain the words "for you"! It must necessarily be concluded that, therefore, the omission of either "for you" or "for many" in a particular rite does not mean that it fails to convey the "vital signification" of the unity of the mystical Body of Christ (otherwise, these two eastern Catholic rites would not be valid) as Mr. Omlor claims is missing from the N.O.M. with its use of "for you and for all" in the vernacular. Therefore, this particular argument against the validity of the N.O.M. used by Omlor and others has no sound basis.

The Use of "ALL" in Eastern Rites

Along with Mr. Omlor, there are others who put forth the erroneous opinion that no other rites have ever used the word "all" in their consecration formulas. In his work, *The Problems with the New Mass*

(Rockford, IL: Tan Books and Publishers, 1990. p. 55), Dr. Rama Coomaraswamy is factually incorrect wherein he states:

> Moreover, of the various Mass rites which the Church has traditionally always recognized as valid - some 76 different rites in many different languages, many of which date back to Apostolic times- NOT ONE has ever used "all" in the form of the consecration of the wine."

The same mistake is put forth by the sedevacantist Peter Dimond in his work against the New Mass wherein he states:

> "no liturgy that has ever been approved by the Church has used the word "all" in the Formula of Consecration" (from web site article: *Short, Irrefutable and Devastating proof from a new angle that the word "all" in place of "many" renders the New Mass invalid*)

Not so gentlemen. Below you will see that there are three Eastern Rites that use (or have used) "all" in the sacramental form as referring to those who receive the benefits of the Holy Sacrifice. In two of these rites, we are provided in the text itself what "all" signifies; and this is precisely what is being argued here, only that the faithful must understand it in accordance with Catholic teaching just as we must do with other parts of the Mass.

- THE ANAPHORA OF ST. JOHN THE APOSTLE AND EVANGELIST.

> "This is the chalice of my blood of the New Testament: Take, drink ye of it: this is shed forth for the life of the world, for the expiation of transgressions, the remission of sins to ALL that believe in him forever and ever."

- THE ANAPHORA OF ST. MARK THE EVANGELIST.

> "This is my blood of the New Testament: Take, drink ye all of it, for the remission of sins of you and of ALL the true faithful, and for eternal life."

We can see with these two examples that in the former "to all" is used, and in the latter "of all" is used in reference to whom the Sacrifice (and its fruits) are applied. The difference is that these two rites provide the Catholic understanding in the text itself. This fact alone demonstrates for us that it is not illegitimate to understand the words "for all" as meaning precisely all of the Elect, or all those upon whom the shed Blood of Christ us efficacious. It also proves that the clause "for all" can, in fact, signify the proper, and thus does not necessitate a signification contrary to Catholic teaching.

Maybe most damaging to the anti-"for all" advocates is the fact that the clause "for all" was used for a number of centuries in one of the old Maronite Canons (they call it the "Anaphoras"). In this ancient Sacred Liturgy there were traditionally 22 Anaphoras. Of these twenty-two Anaphoras, some being perhaps the most ancient in the history of the Church, there are just six still in general use among Maronites at this time. In one of these, the Consecration of the wine did not say "for many." It said "shed for you and for all." For over 300 years this Maronite Anaphora used the Syriac (or Aramaic) translation of the Old Latin text; and in the consecration of the wine in that translation they used the words "for all." This fact is confirmed by two sources.

> "The translation of the old Latin texts said: 'For All.' The original Syriac texts from our liturgy [was] translated 'For Many.' In our recently updated translation, more faithful to the original Syriac, we now have: 'For you and for many.'"
> -Chorbishop Hector Doueihi, Eparchial Liturgist, Brooklyn, NY

> "[M]y old Maronite liturgical books indeed do say in the Consecration 'For All.' In our recent versions, this has been changed to 'For you and for many.' Your point is interesting and well-taken."
> -Father Richard Saad, St. Elias Maronite Church, Birmingham, AL
> (from a private correspondence with an associate of the author)

The Consecration of the wine in the ancient Maronite Canon (which itself was a Syriac translation of the Latin) reads as follows:

"This is the chalice of my blood of the new and eternal Testament which shall be shed for you and for all unto the remission of sin."

This translation was used legitimately and validly and appropriately, without censure from Rome, but with approval. I am not talking about Modern English translations here. The vernacular has never been used in a Maronite Consecration, but always the Aramaic (also called Syriac). The translation was from Latin into Syriac/Aramaic. Their vernacular being, of course, Arabic (in which the REST of the Mass is said). The updated ("Novus Ordo") translations into the world's vernaculars still has its Consecrations in Syriac/Aramaic. Mr. Omlor, though dealing with an English translation of the Maronite Rite (pp. 160-162), conveniently does not address this fact which refutes his entire argument.

This fact alone proves that the wording in the Novus Ordo English translations do not invalidate the Consecration of the wine and thus invalidate the entire Mass.

By the fact that we simply have to understand "for all" in the N.O.M. translations as having the Catholic meaning which two of the above rites provide does not therefore mean the new rite is made null and invalid, or even made suspect. For this same supplied understanding had to be done with the Maronite Rite. Also, by the very fact that, as will be proven below, we have to provide a Catholic understanding to numerous words and clauses in all the Traditional Catholic Rites, both east and west, proves validity is not brought into question, let alone nullified, simply because it has to be done for prayers belonging to the N.O.M. In fact, we are obligated to understand sacramental forms in their Catholic sense, and not in any other sense, and this applies not only to the new form, but also to all traditional forms.

Christ Died for All Men

The reader may notice that in refuting the arguments which hold that the use of "for all" raises doubts as to the validity of the N.O.M., if not nullifies it entirely, we have not done so based on the argument (and defined dogma) that the Lord Jesus died for all men. In other words, we are not arguing that since Our Lord died for all men that therefore the "for all" translation is valid. Those who have attempted to defend the N.O.M. and its translation using "for all" in the Consecration of the wine because Our Lord did die for all men are mistaken in arguing this way. As mentioned on page nine above, the Church also teaches that at that moment in the Holy Sacrifice of the Mass (at the Consecration) Our Lord was referring to the efficacious application of His shed Blood, which, obviously, is not upon all men, since not all men receive the benefit of His death as the Church has dogmatically defined. (St. Thomas Aquinas gives witness to this teaching –that the Mass is concerned with the efficacious application of Christ's Passion- in his *Summa Th.*, III, Q.78, Art. 3.) Thus, to argue that the use of "for all" in the translations of the N.O.M. is proper *because* Our Lord died for all, is incorrect.

Next we will examine the principle of supplied Catholic understanding as applied to liturgical prayers and sacramental forms -both new and traditional. We also will further examine # 3 mentioned above (p. 11 top) which deals with the signification of the effect (or reality) of the Sacrament, viz., union with the Mystical Body- in both Part III and Part V of this critique.

POINT II:

PRINCIPLE OF SUPPLIED CATHOLIC UNDERSTANDING

There is a principle in Catholic theology which states that the terms of ecclesiastical formulas, whether dogmatic or sacramental, must be understood in light of constant orthodox Catholic teaching and doctrine. This is known as the supplied Catholic understanding (or signification) of terms and clauses. Understanding terms in this way is also known as understanding them with the *Sensus Fidei*, the sense of the (Catholic) Faith. At Vatican Council I, the Church infallibly declared that what she puts forth is "to be believed and held by all the faithful *according to the ancient and continual faith of the Universal Church*" (Pastor Aeternus, Denz: 1821 [DS: 3052]; italics added). Therefore, we are to understand the new sacramental form of the N.O.M. "according to the ancient and continual faith of the Universal Church."

The Church, then, requires the faithful to understand the approved new sacramental form, as she does for all the others, according to Catholic teaching, according to what she means by the terms. So the words "for all" can be (and *must* be) understood in an orthodox manner as meaning for ALL the members of the Body of Christ, or for ALL those upon whom the Blood of Jesus is efficacious, and not as for all men of all time, implying the heresy of universal salvation. Since we are, in fact, able to interpret the words of the new formula "according to the ancient and continual faith of the Universal Church," it necessarily follows that the words "for all" do not necessitate an unorthodox meaning, or a meaning contrary to Sacred Tradition concerning the purpose and efficacy of the Sacrifice of the Mass as Mr. Omlor and others suppose. The supplied Catholic understanding provides for us what these words do mean in the sacramental form. And this is precisely what we have to do with other words and clauses within both the traditional Rite and in many of the Eastern Rites. We will look at some significant examples of this below. But first a few objections this author has come across need to be answered.

OBJECTION I: But the intentional mistranslation of *pro multis* by liberals affects the Sacrament itself.

ANSWER: The mistranslation, intentional or not, has no effect on the confecting of the Sacrament itself, by the fact that this has no intrinsic effect upon the words themselves, for the words "for all" do not *necessitate* a meaning contrary to Catholic teaching on this point in the Mass. This objection erroneously presumes that the new words necessarily signify something other than all upon whom the Precious Blood is efficacious. On the contrary, it has been proven that they do not necessitate a meaning contrary to Catholic teaching. Besides, those liberal fools cannot invalidate and nullify God's action as easily as they think or wish (or as easily as some legalistic radical traditionalists think).

Now, it may (but not necessarily so) cause a misleading didactic effect upon the faithful who, when hearing the words "for all," may interpret these words differently from what the Church understands by them. However, this happens with many dogmas of Holy Mother Church because of poor catechesis. But how people understand it or interpret it has nothing to do with the truth itself and *what the Church means by said words*. In our case with "for all," how people understand it has nothing to do with that which the Church understands by these words or intends to do with the act.

If anything, it is the effect of poor catechesis that can cause an understanding of "for all" to be contrary to what the Church really teaches and intends. Thus, the real problem is in the realm of catechesis, of how poorly the Faith is being taught, and this results in a lack of Catholic faith among those baptized as Catholics and who attend Holy Mass. The Faith in all its purity has not been properly taught for the last generation or more. Hence the sound principle: dogma comes before liturgy.

The problems concerning the new form and its translation in the vernacular came to the attention not only of the Sacred Congregation for

Divine Worship, but also of the Sacred Congregation for the Doctrine of the Faith (SCDF, for short). This is so, because the proper (or improper) interpretation of sacramental forms is a matter of the Faith. In 1974, the SCDF sent out a letter to all the episcopal conferences, *Insauratio Liturgica* (25 January, 1974), known as the "Declaration on the Meaning of Translations of Sacramental Formulae," (published in the Notitiae, January, 1974, No. 80). In this declaration the Sacred Congregation recognizes that translations into modern languages have:

> given rise to certain difficulties, which have come to light now that the translations have been sent by episcopal conferences to the Holy See for approval. In these circumstances, the Sacred Congregation for the Doctrine of the Faith again calls attention to the necessity that the essential formulae of the sacramental rites render faithfully the original sense of the Latin "typical text." With that in mind it declares:

> When a vernacular translation of a sacramental formula is submitted to the Holy See for approval, it examines it carefully. When it is satisfied that it expresses the meaning intended by the Church, it approves and confirms it, stipulating, however, that *it must be understood in accordance with the mind of the Church as expressed in the original Latin text.* (italics added)

We see here that the SCDF is declaring that the translations must be understood according to the mind of the Church as expressed in the original Latin text. This is the principle of supplied Catholic understanding, in conformity to the Decree, *Pastor Aeternus*, of Vatican I (quoted above), being required for the faithful. Thus, just as the words "for many" can be (and must be) understood as the 'many' who make up the members of the Mystical Body of Christ, or the 'many' upon whom the Blood of Christ is efficacious, so must the words "for all" be understood as meaning 'all' upon whom the blood of Christ is efficacious, which is many men.

OBJECTION II: We know that Our Lord Jesus Christ said "for many" at the Last Supper. It is in the Gospels. Yet, those defending "for all" are engaging in the same word games that the liberals use to undermine the holy dogmas of the Church.

ANSWER: No we are not engaging in word games. We simply understand the words of the new formula "according to the ancient and continual faith of the Universal Church," as the Church demands of the faithful. Any honest and right reasoned person will admit the fact that "for all" could mean and, when understood "according to the ancient and continual faith of the Universal Church" concerning the Mass, does mean the following:

- for all members of the Mystical Body of Christ; or
- for all upon whom the Christ's shed Blood is efficacious; or
- for all who hold the Catholic Faith.

(Read your traditional Latin/Roman Rite offertory carefully, all of these categories are in fact mentioned among the intentions for the sacrificial offering). To put it another way, logic and grammar demand that we admit that "for all" does not exclude these. IF one can at the least be honest enough and admit that "for all" can mean any (and all) of these, THEN you should recognize that it necessarily follows that:

1. "For all" does not change the meaning of what Our Lord spoke, therefore there is no change in signification;
2. "For all" is even consistent with the offering of the traditional Rite, let alone the new Rite;
3. No word games are involved, for this very same "exercise" is done with a number of other words/phrases in the traditional Rites, both eastern and western (see below); and besides, we are required to understand these formulas "according to the ancient and continual faith of the Universal Church" (Vatican I).

Does this mean that we are saying that *pro multis* should have been translated as "for all"? No, not at all, for that is an incorrect translation. But thanks to the protective action of the Holy Spirit over the Church, the words "for all" do not necessitate a change in signification with the new sacramental form in its translation.

OBJECTION III: But, if one were required to provide a meaning, then by that very necessity the new wording has changed the meaning as previously stated, or a provided meaning would not be necessary.

ANSWER: This objection presumes and applies that which is illogical, as well as fails to take into account what the Church at Vatican I demands of the faithful. Let us look at this logically:

    1. To provide a meaning (or interpretation) to a word (or clause) does not necessitate that said word has changed the meaning of that which it replaced. It MAY in other contexts change the meaning, but it does not necessarily do such here. And we are talking of necessity, here. The arguments against validity of the N.O.M. depend on necessity, but they do not have it (see Point III below).

    2. The need for and fact of providing a meaning to a word or clause does not *necessarily* mean that a corruption has occurred; because as we shall see from a number of examples from the Traditional Latin/Roman Rite, we ARE required to provide a proper (orthodox Catholic) meaning to certain words and clauses within the traditional Latin Mass, and we know there are no inherent corruptions within this Rite. Besides, as just proven above, it is the teaching of the Church that ALL the faithful believe and hold (i.e. understand/interpret) these terms "according to the ancient and continual faith of the Universal Church."

OBJECTION IV: But it is this changed meaning which is at the heart of the *De Defectibus* prescription that: "If anyone removes or changes anything in the Form of the Consecration of the Body and Blood, and by this change of words, does not signify the same thing AS THESE WORDS DO, he does not confect the Sacrament".

ANSWER: But when understood in light of Catholic teaching the words "for all" can and do signify the very same thing as these words "for many" do. Thus, the prescription cited here from *De Defectibus* does not apply. It would apply ONLY if the different words in fact brought about a change in signification, but they do not. No such change is necessitated by the new formula as demonstrated.

OBJECTION V: Just by the fact that the mistranslation would call for a supplied understanding indicates at least a doubt concerning signification and that this new wording "does not signify the same thing as these words (the proper ones) do".

ANSWER: No, this is not so, for I have demonstrated that above. The changing of "for many" into "for all" does not necessitate a change in meaning (or change in signification) for two reasons:

    A. precisely because it *can* be understood to mean for all the Elect, or for all who are cleansed by the Precious Blood of Christ, and does mean such when supplied a Catholic understanding, as Vatican I demands; and

    B. because "all" has been used in the Anaphoras of three Eastern Catholic Rites and was accepted as valid.

Let us recognize this point: Vatican I infallibly defined (*De Fide Definita*) that Right Reason and the Faith can never contradict one another, but are always consistent; and also that Right Reason can reach certain truths outside the bounds of ecclesiastical promulgation (cf. Denz. 1797, 1799 [DS. 3017, 3019]). The principle of necessity, properly applied, proves that the N.O. Consecration is, at the least, not invalid, hence its validity since this is an either/or proposition.

OBJECTION VI: Well, something has changed or you would not now need to provide an understanding (for validity) that was not previously necessary for validity.

ANSWER: This question reveals a total ignorance concerning the fact that a supplied Catholic understanding is employed with numerous terms and formulas in every Rite. At the same time, of course something has changed, the N.O. is a new/different Rite. But this objection presumes that which is erroneous. It presumes that validity is dependent upon how we understand certain words. Validity is NOT dependent upon how some individuals understand "for all," or even "This is my body." Dear God, Our Lord would never have His divine/sacred action depend upon such a subjective basis. The dependency of validity is upon the actual meanings of the words *as the Church uses and understands them*, not whether or not individuals understand certain words one way or another. Rather, we must conform our understanding to that which the Church applies to them.

Anyway, we have to provide an understanding for words and phrases in line with Catholic orthodoxy in places in numerous other Rites, as well as in the traditional Rite, yet this has no effect on validity.

OBJECTION VII: The liberals simply introduce ambiguity into what once had been clear and count on the "conservative" to give the ambiguity an orthodox interpretation while hiding behind feigned virtue of obedience.

ANSWER: This means nothing as to the words themselves. The traditional Rites, Western and Eastern, are only clear to those who have been catechized properly. In fact, we must give orthodox interpretations to other parts of the traditional Latin Canon itself and this does not cause a doubt concerning their validity. Let us look at the words "for you and for many." These words are not as clear in and of themselves concerning their sacramental signification as many think. These also require a supplied Catholic understanding.

FOR YOU AND FOR MANY AND SUPPLIED CATHOLIC UNDERSTANDING

Throughout his book Mr. Omlor goes to great pains to spell out the Catholic meaning of the words "for you and for many." He quotes St. Thomas Aquinas more often than any other source. The fact that St. Thomas and Mr. Omlor must write out the Catholic understanding of the words "for you and for many," proves my point that even within the traditional Rite we must supply a Catholic understanding to words which do not convey in and of themselves such a meaning as regards their Catholic/sacramental signification. Thus, this principle of supplying a Catholic understanding is valid and therefore cannot be denied when having to apply it to words and phrase in the new Mass, particularly "for all."

1. "FOR YOU"

Is it really clear as to what exactly these words mean; that is, to whom they refer? Do they address and include all the Apostles? Most people think so. But they do not. Why not, you might ask? Here's why: because

Judas was still there (see Gospel of St. Luke 22: stated after institution verses: 19ff). Yet the Mass is the *efficacious* application of Christ's shed Blood, but it was not efficacious for Judas. Thus, Judas could not be included in the words "for you" even though he was right there and was a part of the twelve to whom Our Lord was addressing. We know that Judas was present at the Consecration because we know he was a bishop. Acts 1:20 makes this clear, where it is declared that "another must take his [Judas'] bishopric." God's Word infallibly declares that Judas was a bishop. Now, only priests can be bishops, and the Church has defined as dogma that the priesthood was established by Christ when he declared after the Consecration: "Do this for a commemoration of me." (Trent, "On the Most Holy Sacrifice of the Mass," Chap.1, Canon 1; see Denz.938, 949)

Therefore, Judas was present, but was not included when Christ said "for you."

Now, because the Holy Sacrifice of the Mass is the efficacious application of the merits of Christ's shed Blood, it necessarily follows that despite being right there at the Last Supper with Our Lord, Judas could not have been included in the words "for you," even though in the Greek the "you" is in the plural. We know this to be true since Judas allowed Satan to enter into him (Lk.22:3), and neither cooperated with the graces from the first Mass (the Last Supper), nor did he persevere to the end, as he hung himself thereby being guilty of mortal sin. Therefore, since we know Judas was not included in "for you," the following necessarily follows:

A. Our Lord uses a term which in appearance is all-inclusive to those whom He addresses, but in fact is not all-inclusive. The same must be allowed for "for all" in the N.O.M., if one is to be consistent. As Our Lord can never be misleading, therefore the use of "for all" is not necessarily misleading.

B. The words "for you" do have a degree of ambiguity, IF it is exact-precision one wants. Therefore, some degree of ambiguity exists even in undisputed words, which thus means that ambiguity does not preclude validity nor cause validity to be doubted. However, no ambiguity exists when one sees "for you" (and "for all)" in light of Catholic teaching, and that is my point.

Therefore, there can be and are men not included in "for all," since Our Lord just used a term which by appearance was inclusive, but was in fact not.

2. "FOR MANY"

Now look at the words, "for many." These also are not as clear as many presume. Sacramental theology tells us that these two words signify the members of the Mystical Body of Christ. Wow! They do? Yes, they do. But it necessarily follows that they signify such only by supplying a Catholic interpretation to them. It is clear that *in and of themselves* they signify no such thing. Even in the context of the institution narrative and the consecration formula they, in and of themselves, do not clearly signify the members of Christ's Body.

Ask yourself: do the words "for many" clearly indicate the members of the Mystical Body of Christ? Are we told right there in the text that "for many" is in reference to whom? No, we are not. The two words "for many" are not explicit as to which many:

a. Is it for the many who are baptized (since not all men of all time are baptized)?
b. Is it for the many who are baptized AND who hold the true Faith and are not separated from Christ's Vicar? or,
c. Is it for the many who receive the benefits of Christ's shed blood upon the cross?

Do the words "for many" stand for only *many of the Elect*, or for the *many who are the Elect*? Do they stand for only many of those upon whom the shed blood of Christ is efficacious, or for the many upon whom the blood of Christ is efficacious? Which is it? How is the term to be understood? The text itself does not make this clear. Only a supplied Catholic understanding makes it clear; and that is the point being presented here.

Think about this point in reference to the last question: Our Lord elsewhere said, *many* are called but only *few* are chosen (Matt.22:14). Now, at the Consecration, Our Lord says "for many." So does Our Lord now mean MORE than only the few who are chosen will receive the efficacious application of His shed blood? Do not the few who are chosen mean the Elect? Since Christ now says "for many," as distinct from the few who are chosen from the many called, does Our Lord now mean more than the Elect, and thus mean all who are justified (for not all who are justified are part of the Elect, since not all who are justified persevere to the end)? Or does He now use this term in a different sense than before? Which of these is it? Our Lord says neither specifically or explicitly which, and the text of even the traditional canon fails to make this clear.

Therefore, the very same exercise of needing to supply an orthodox Catholic understanding to "for all" must also be engaged with both the clauses "for you" and "for many." It is the same principle, the same exercise. The same necessity to apply the principle exists in all the traditional rites. Yet, this does not at all invalidate nor call into question the validity of the traditional rites and their sacramental forms. Therefore, the employment of this principle of supplying a Catholic meaning in the New Mass is valid, proper, and consistent with tradition. In fact, it is necessary to supply such Catholic meanings to these terms as I proved at the beginning of Point II above. We shall now look at numerous other applications of this principle.

APPLYING THE PRINCIPLE OF SUPPLIED UNDERSTANDING TO THE TRADITIONAL LITURGY

Here are some more examples from both the Traditional Latin/Roman Rite itself and from some Eastern Rite liturgies wherein this principle of supplied understanding must be employed, otherwise heretical under-standings could, in fact, result.

1. Look at the traditional offertory wherein it is prayed:

"OFFERIMUS TIBI, DOMINUS.... TOTIUS MUNDI SALUTE."

28

Here, the priest states that the chalice is offered up for "our salvation and for the WHOLE WORLD" (some translations have "for ALL the world"). Yet, this cannot be promoting the heresy of universal salvation, since we know that the Holy Sacrifice of the Mass is the *efficacious* application of Christ's shed Blood, and the "whole world" is neither saved, nor even justified. Therefore, it MUST be understood in light of Catholic theology/orthodoxy, that is, for all the members of the Mystical Body throughout the whole world. And this understanding must be supplied. (If one argues that the sufficiency of Christ's death is what is being referred to at this point here in the liturgy, then it means that that understanding must still be supplied at that point in the liturgy, and THAT also substantiates my point.)

2. After the consecration the Sacred Body is called "bread" (that's right!), the "bread of eternal life." Yet we know it is no longer bread and not promoting the heresy of Eucharistic symbolism. Therefore, it must be understood in light of Catholic theology/orthodoxy. Cardinal Borromeo's Commission which drew up the Catechism of Trent had to spend an entire paragraph explaining why the consecrated Host was still called "bread" *after* the Consecration, precisely because such phraseology could lead the faithful into heresy. Hence, the necessity of supplied Catholic understanding.

3. After the consecration the priest asks God the Father to accept "these sacrifices" (plural). But there is only one sacrifice being offered here, the sacrifice of Christ on Calvary. There are not multiple sacrifices being offered, for this would be the heresy of which Protestants have historically accused the true Church, since Christ died once for all. Plural is not equated with singular in everyday concepts, however, here in the Sacred Liturgy it is. Therefore, we are required to understand this in light of Catholic teaching. (One may say that at this point the priest is including the faithful in union with Christ and offering themselves up with Him. But it doesn't *say that* in the text, thus it can only be understood as such with an informed Catholic understanding)

4. The Canon for Holy Thursday reads: "Who, on the day before He suffered for our salvation and that of *all men*, that is, this day, took bread into His holy and venerable hands...." (St. Pius X, Daily Missal, 1956;

29

italics added). Here we do find the words "all men" in a traditional canon. Does this prayer imply, if not explicitly state, that the Holy Sacrifice of the Mass is being offered for (and thus efficacious for) all men of all time? It sure can be (mis)understood to mean such by some. But the answer is, no. When the Catholic understanding is supplied, then we know this is not what is being implied here. It can only mean that this sacrifice offered for all those upon whom the precious blood is efficacious. Hence, the necessity of supplied Catholic understanding here.

5. In the Mass for the Dead, the Church prays for the departed as though they were still capable of being rescued from the gates of Hell. But we know this cannot be true. Hence the validity and necessity of supplying the proper understanding.

Eastern Catholic Rites

6. In the Eastern Liturgies there is a prayer which is called the *Epiclesis*. This prayer invokes the Holy Spirit to "make this bread the precious Body of Christ, and that which is in this chalice, the precious blood of Thy Christ." But this prayer is said *after* the consecrations, which means that the sacred body and precious blood of Christ are already present, for this is dogma. So this prayer gives the apparent understanding that Transubstantiation has not yet occurred, but it has. Therefore, this prayer requires that the Catholic supply a proper Catholic/sacramental understanding to it.

7. In the Divine Liturgy of St. John Chrysostom (the primary liturgy of the Byzantine Rite), at the minor elevation, which is immediately following the consecration of the wine, the priests prays: "We offer to You Yours of Your own, in behalf of all AND FOR ALL." In light of proper Catholic theology we know this must mean for all members of the Mystical Body, or for all of the Elect. Otherwise, the heresy of universal salvation is implied since the Mass is the efficacious application of Christ's merits gained upon the cross. Hence, the necessity of supplied Catholic understanding.

8. In this same Sacred Liturgy, soon after the Consecration, there appears this prayer: "Look down from Heaven, O Master, upon those who have bowed their heads to You, for they have not bowed them down to flesh and blood, but to You the awesome God." Here it appears that, even though the very Body and Blood of Christ is Present, there is a rejection of the Real Presence. That they do not bow down to Christ's flesh and blood, inseparable from his divinity. But of course, we know this is not what is being stated here. Hence, the necessity of supplying a Catholic understanding to this prayer.

More examples could be provided. But the point, the principle is established. ALL of these require that certain words and phrases be understood in light of Catholic teaching since they could also be misinterpreted to mean something contrary to Catholic teaching. As with these and other words and clauses from traditional liturgies, so a Catholic understanding must be supplied to the words "for all" in the N.O.M. Therefore by both reason and the principle of usage employed in traditional rites:

• the words "for all" do not invalidate the consecration, because when supplied with a Catholic understanding they do signify the effect of the application of the fruits of His passion -to ALL the Elect.

• the need to provide a Catholic understanding to "for all" does not legitimize doubt concerning the validity of the new Consecration form.

So the fact is that in all the rites there is a Catholic understanding that MUST be supplied in order to keep out of heresy and harm's way. It has been this way since Day One, and such "understanding" must be supplied at times even to the infallible words of Holy Scripture. How else, as shown before, do we explain the many places in which the Bible says that "all" men are sinners, knowing that Jesus and His Blessed Mother are, in fact, men, but not sinners?

Authoritative Statements

OBJECTION VIII: One might bring up the objection that Mr. Omlor points out that this very question concerning why "for all" could not be used has already been addressed by St. Thomas Aquinas (Summa Theologica, Pt. III, Q.78, A.3), by St. Alphonsus Ligouri in his "Treatise on the Holy Eucharist," by the Catechism of the of Trent (produced under the supervision of St. Charles Borromeo, and published under Pope St. Pius V), and by Pope Benedict XIV, who quotes St. Thomas above in his work, "The Most Holy Sacrifice of the Mass" (Book II, Chap. XV, par.11). Everyone of these specifically state that Christ did not use the word "all" because "all" would refer to the sufficiency of His Passion; and in the institution of this sacrament Christ used the word "many" because He was specifically referring to the efficacy of His Passion.

Therefore the claim that the words, "for all" can be (and must be) understood in an orthodox manner as meaning for ALL members of the Body of Christ, or for ALL of the Elect" is in direct contradiction to everyone of these authorities.

ANSWER: No this claim is not in direct contradiction, nor in indirect contradiction to these authoritative sources, either. This objection is missing an important point. Each of these authorities worked on the presumption of "for all" as being understood as for all men of all time, as if these words necessitated a reference to the virtue of the Sacrament (i.e., its sufficiency) and not its fruit (i.e., its efficiency). However, I am dealing with a principle which NONE of these authorities explicitly addressed, but nonetheless, assumed and employed: that of supplied Catholic understanding (as required by Vatican I and the SCDF -Objection I above). This principle of supplied Catholic understanding they all accepted since it must be applied in other places within the traditional Latin/Roman Rite, as well as in other rites. The very principle itself must also be used on both "for you" as well as "for many" as previously shown. They would not have had to comment at all on this matter if this principle did not also have to be applied to "for many."

The explanations offered by the above sources deal with what Our Lord stated and why He did not use "for all," precisely because "for many" must also be understood in accordance with Catholic teaching. These terms and clauses require that a meaning be given/understood in accordance with orthodox Catholic teaching.

Two more points:

1. St. Thomas Aquinas, and therefore both Pope Benedict XIV and St. Alphonsus De Liguori who quote St. Thomas on this matter, was dealing with the objection which states that "for all" should be used in the Consecration to refer to the sufficiency of Christ's Sacrifice on the cross, not its efficacy. So none of these authorities actually deal with the particular matter being addressed here: that for all" can be understood in reference to the efficacy of Christ's Sacrifice as applying to ALL upon whom the shed Blood is efficacious.

2. These authorities all dealt with "for all" only in its sense as meaning/signifying something other than many; but they did not exclude any other sense as belonging to "for all." Also, none of these authorities declared that the words "for all" cannot in any way be understood as referring to the efficacy of Christ's Passion upon all the elect. Therefore, these authorities do not address the real substance and essence of the current issue, and thus cannot be used against this defense of the validity of the N.O.M. with the use of "for all."

OBJECTION IX: Christ, being incapable of lying, could "never" have said "for all," having the infallible knowledge that all men would never avail themselves of His sacrifice.

ANSWER: Of course Our Lord could never deceive. But "for all" does not necessitate this interpretation as demonstrated above. However He could very well have said "for all," meaning ALL of the Elect, or all the members of His Mystical Body.

Think about it this way: The words "for many" could be misconstrued as meaning not *all* of the Elect, but only *many*, and this would be heretical. Thus one could construe these words of our Lord in a way contrary to what the Church understands and thus claim that Christ used deceiving language. Do you see? It works both ways. Thus the words "for all" are in line with orthodox Catholic teaching concerning the Mass as being understood as applying to ALL for whom the benefits of Christ's shed blood is efficacious. These facts are really quite easy to see once the principle of supplied Catholic understanding is recognized and employed.

Is the New Mass of Pope Paul VI Invalid?

POINT III:

PRINCIPLE OF LOGICAL NECESSITY

It has been mentioned already in this work that the argument of defect in form put forth by Mr. Omlor and others depends upon the principle of necessity in that "for all" necessarily means, that is can ONLY mean, that which is contrary to Catholic teaching. But Mr. Omlor, et al, do not have it at all. "For all" does not necessarily mean what they say it must mean. And, as previously pointed out, the law cited from *De Defectibus* does not apply to "for all." It would apply ONLY if the different words do in fact make a change in signification, but no such necessity of change exists as demonstrated. Thus, the defect of form proponents (in regards to "for all") lack the necessity of changed meaning/signification they NEED in order for their arguments of invalidity to be, well... valid and true.

Since this is an "either/or" situation, therefore, the defect in form argument fails to disprove validity of the N.O. Mass; hence the validity of the NO Mass/Consecration.

In his work, "Questioning the Validity of the Mass Using the New, All-English Canon" (# 110 ff; page 38 in *The Robber Church*), Mr. Omlor changes the very question concerning the reality of the sacrament. He asks, "Do *all men* belong to the Mystical Body?" (italics in the original) But this is NOT the question. We know that all men do not, nor will ever, belong to the Mystical Body of Christ. Mr. Omlor misleads his readers by phrasing the question, and thus the issue, this way. However, the question, the issue is NOT, as Mr. Omlor asks, to "ascertain whether ALL MEN can be considered members of the Body of Christ" (# 111, p.38), but whether or not the WORDS "for all (men)" of the new sacramental form necessarily convey or imply a universally inclusive meaning/sense of all men belonging to the Body of Christ. We have proven that they do not (Points I and II above), and this lack of necessity works against Mr. Omlor's position. (We have also proven that these words can easily have an orthodox meaning, and that we must understand them as such.)

Also, the terms in a sacramental form, because they require a Catholic-sacramental understanding, often have a technical meaning not usually understood with its common usage, but he fails to admit or address this fact. This is precisely why we must understand sacramental forms as the Church understands and uses them. Again, it is required of the faithful to understand sacramental forms in their Catholic sense, and not in any other possible sense.

OBJECTION I: But do not those who defend the use of "for all" depend also upon the principle of necessity? In other words, isn't it also true that "for all" must necessarily mean 'for all those upon whom the blood of Christ is efficacious' for it to remain valid?

ANSWER: No, the defense of "for all" does not depend upon the principle of necessity. Only those who deny the legitimate use of "for all" depend upon necessity. There are at least two reasons why this is so, and each alone proves the position.

Reason # 1. As demonstrated already, the words "for you…" do not necessarily mean for everyone of those who were present when Our Lord spoke those words at the Last Supper, because Judas was there; nor do the words "for many" necessarily of themselves mean or indicate those upon whom the blood of Christ is efficacious, or for all the elect of the Mystical Body of Christ. Yet, the lack of necessity with these words does not invalidate the Holy Sacrifice of the Mass. It is the Church that supplies signification to these words as meaning such. IF logical necessity of a Catholic meaning were required for the words "for all," THEN it would also be required for the words "for many." But the words "for many" do not necessitate a Catholic meaning in and of themselves (which is precisely why St. Thomas and Mr. Omlor spent much ink in explaining the Catholic understanding of the words "for you and for many"), therefore there would be no valid Masses in any Rite since these words do not necessitate an orthodox meaning either. Of course, this cannot be held.

Therefore, logical necessity is not needed for the words "for all," since they are not needed for the clause "for you and for many," for we cannot have two different and contrary requirements involved in sacramental forms. Thus, because we know that the traditional rites use words that do not necessitate in and of themselves meanings which the Church supplies for them, yet are still valid, this proves that logical necessity is not needed in defense of the new Rite. This alone proves that the principle of necessity is required only upon those who deny the validity of the N.O.M. based upon the change in the form from "for you and for many unto the remission of sin" to "for you and for all the forgiveness of sins." The necessity is required only for those who negate (i.e., deny) validity.

Reason # 2. Necessity is not required of the "for all" defense because logic is not a two-way street; it functions only on a one-way street. In other words, it functions only in one direction at a time. Those who deny validity based on the changed sacramental form hold a position that is negative in nature. This is so even if it is stated in a grammatically positive form: i.e., "The N.O.M. IS invalid because the new form signifies an essential change in meaning and thus it suppresses what is essential and signifies falsely." This is still a position that is negative in nature: i.e., it denies validity.

The anti-"for all" position is itself invalid because it depends upon arguments which themselves are based upon a construct which does not necessitate that which is contrary to Catholic teaching (i.e. "for all" does not necessarily mean that which is contrary to Catholic teaching); therefore their conclusion does not necessarily follow. The anti-valid position depends upon arguments that are based upon a non-necessitated meaning: i.e., that "for all" only means "for all men who ever lived." In other words, the arguments against "for all" depend upon the notion that these words necessarily signify that which is contrary to Church teaching on the efficacious application of the merits of Christ death upon the Elect. But, they do not necessarily mean such as already proven. They also erroneously presume that "for all" can in no way mean for all upon whom the blood of Christ is efficacious, or for all the Elect.

Let me demonstrate why logic and necessity work only in one direction. Let's put the pattern of the argument in the abstract first:

Formula A:
If a, then b.
The proposition "b" always necessarily follows from "a."

However, it does not necessarily follow that:
If b, then a; for logic is only a one way street.

Therefore: If a, then b, but NOT if b, then a.

Now let's use a concrete example of these equations:
IF it rains (a), THEN the ground will be wet (b): if a, then b.

However it does not follow that:

IF the ground is wet (b), THEN it has rained (a):

Here we see that the equation -if b, then a(of the above)- does not necessarily follow. Why? Well, someone could have watered their yard, or washed their car, or there could have been a water-main break, or what ever. Thus, the ground being wet does not necessitate that it rained. So, IF the ground is wet (b), THEN it does not necessarily mean that it rained (a) to make it wet.

*Do not read on until you have understood this important fact of logic.

Hopefully you can now see that logic and the principle of logical necessity work only in one direction. At the same time, if you negate both a and b and start from the other direction, then the logic/necessity still works, but now it heads in the opposite direction (still one way, though). Therefore negated in the abstract it reads as thus:

Formula B:
If not-b, then not-a (that is, if a, then b)(remember: a=rain, b= wet ground)

Negated in the concrete it is thus:

IF the ground is NOT wet (if not-b), THEN it has not rained (then not-a).

We can see here that if both are negated and then reversed, then logical necessity does follow. Of course, these logical equations depend upon the premise as being true. You cannot say: If a, then b, whereby "a" is hot and "b" is the South Pole: If it is hot (a), then the location is Antarctica (b). This does not follow since the premise is wrong.

Try these logical equations on any scenario, where the premise is true, and it will always, always, with no exceptions, work this way. This is an absolute.

Let's apply this concretely to the Mass:
A. If a, then b= If the sacramental form signifies something different (a), then the sacrament is invalid (b).

Remember, logic works only one way, so, as just shown, we know that the above does not work in the opposite direction:

B. If b, then not necessarily a= If the sacrament is invalid (b), then it is not necessarily because the form signified something different (a).

Why is this so? Well, invalidity could also be the result of improper matter, or a man without Holy Orders, or improper intent. Again, logic works in only one direction. Now, let's negate both:

Presuming A above (i.e. if the sacramental form signifies something different), we proceed with the logical equation:

If not b, then not-a = If the sacrament is NOT invalid (if not-b), that is, if it is valid, then the form does NOT signify something different (then not-a). This format is always true, no exceptions.

All of this is to provide you, dear reader, with a foundation in correct reasoning (viz. Logic). Those who do not employ logic and right reasoning either start with an erroneous premise or argue incorrectly concerning their position or beliefs.

Now, those who say that the new form does not signify the same as the traditional form depend upon this logical necessity just demonstrated, but their position does not have this necessity. They depend upon "for all" as *necessarily* signifying all men who ever lived, but anyone can see that the words "for all' can mean for all the members of the Mystical Body of Christ; or for all upon whom the Christ's shed Blood is efficacious, AND, when understood in light of Catholic teaching, these words DO signify these meanings. By the very fact that "for all" can signify orthodox meanings it renders these words as not necessitating an UNorthodox meaning.

The anti-valid/doubtful validity proponents depend upon one of the following arguments (or formulas) whereby they say that the N.O.M. is invalid because "for all" changes signification.

• If "for all" is used (a), then all men of all time is signified (b).

-Invalid conclusion. This does not work because the conclusion is in error by the fact that "for all" does not necessarily mean "all men of all time." In other word, the "b" is not necessitated by "a."

• If "for all" is used, then the signification is changed.

-Invalid conclusion. This also does not work because the conclusion is in error by the fact that "for all" does not necessarily change signification as proven in this work. In other words, the "b" is not necessitated by "a."

• If "for all" is used, then the Mass is rendered invalid.

-Invalid conclusion. This also does not work because the conclusion is in error by the fact that "for all" does not necessarily change signification. That is, there is nothing which prohibits "for all" from having the orthodox Catholic meaning of refering to all those upon whom the blood of Christ is efficacious. In other words, the "b" is not necessitated by "a."

These all fail to meet the requirement of necessity. All these erroneous formulas are the basis upon which those who argue "for all" changes signification. Thus, those who deny or doubt the validity of the New Mass based on the use of "for all" actually base their conclusions on two erroneous presumptions:

1. That "for all" necessarily means that which is contrary to proper signification and Catholic teaching (i.e. that it necessarily means all men of all time); and,

2. That "for all" can in no way signify that which is in accord with Catholic teaching (i.e. it cannot be understood to mean "for all upon whom the shed blood of Christ is efficacious).

In these two erroneous presumptions, necessity exists in neither one. Now, a true logical equation reads thus:

IF the use of "for all" renders the sacrament invalid (a), *THEN* it necessitates a change in signification (b). This is true as formulated. But we now know that "for all" does not necessitate a change in signification. We now will use "Formula B" from above where both "a" and "b" are negated, that is where: "a" = the Sacrament is valid, and "b" = "for all" can validly be understood as signifying the same.

If "for all" does not necessitate a meaning contrary to the Church's teaching on the Mass (not-b), then it does not render the sacrament invalid (not-a). It has been proven that "for all" does not necessitate a change in signification (not-b), therefore its use does not render the sacrament invalid (not-a).

THEREFORE, the N.O.M. is not invalid, but is valid.

Let us put this into another logical formula.

IF "for all" can be understood as meaning for all upon whom the shed blood of Christ is efficacious, THEN its use does not render the sacrament invalid. "For all" can be understood as meaning such, because there exists within the words themselves nothing that prohibits such an understanding, therefore the N.O.M. is not invalid, but valid.

As mentioned before, the Church has infallibly defined at Vatican I that Right Reason and Faith (and Revelation) cannot contradict each other, but are consistent (see Denz. 1797, 1799). Thus, the Natural Law of God, found and expressed in Right-Reason, both disproves the anti-"for all" proponents and their arguments, and proves that "for all" does not invalidate the Holy Sacrifice of the Mass.

THE LEONINE PRINCIPLE

Mr. Omlor (pp. 40ff, "The Robber Church") and Father Paul Trinchard ("The Abbot and Me," Maeta, 1997, pp. 127 ff), along with the Dimond brothers ("Short, Irrefutable and Devastating proof from a new angle that the word "all" in place of "many" renders the New Mass invalid," from web site) state that there is a principle involved when Pope Leo XIII solemnly declared Anglican orders as null and void (Apostolicae Curae, 1896). Fr. Trinchard holds that this principle can (and must) be applied to the Novus Ordo Mass (he calls it a "service"). Put briefly, using the words of Pope Leo XIII himself, the principle is this:

> The "form cannot be considered apt or sufficient for the sacrament which omits what it ought essentially to signify." (Apostolicae Curae, par. 27, as quoted in "The Abbot and Me," pp. 131-132)

Fr. Trinchard admits that the words "omits what it ought essentially to signify' is the key phrase (p.132). Earlier he also states that the principle involves not only defective form, but also defect in intention (p.131). Adding one more aspect to the latter, Fr. Trinchard says that what the designers of the NO had in mind and intended when they composed the New Mass (pp. 132-134) must be included.

The fundamental principle involved in Pope Leo XIII condemnation of Anglican orders will not be argued against here. We recognize that a principle exists. The questions are:

•can it successfully be applied to the new Mass?
•Do Fr. Trinchard and Peter Dimond apply it to the new Mass?
• If so, do they thereby prove from the application of this principle to the new Mass that the new Mass is invalid?

Fr. Trinchard indicates by a heading that he will be applying the Leonine Principle to the N.O. Mass (pp.135-144). However, he spends most of the pages immediately following this heading applying it not to the New Mass, but to the new Ordination Rite. In fact, he does not actually apply the principle to the new Mass at this point, but merely states:

> "Obviously, the intelligent and unbiased application of the Leonine Principle upon NOEL (Novus Ordo English Liturgy)... will lead any honest Catholic to personally conclude that since Anglican Liturgy (services and ordinals) were dogmatically declared to be invalid -'null and void'- *a fortiori*, NOEL services and ordinals as actually used and propagated must be 'null and void' or invalid. (pp. 136-137)

Fr. Trinchard then says: "This line of argumentation demonstrates why an increasing number of faithful Catholics are concluding that Novus Ordinals and services [sic] are invalid as well as illicit" (p.137).

The question any logically thinking reader will ask after reading this is: WHAT argumentation? Fr. Trinchard simply states that the "unbiased application of the Leonine Principle upon the NOEL will lead any honest Catholic to personally conclude" that the NOEL liturgy as used must be "null and void." This is no "line of argumentation," let alone proof that when the Leonine Principle is applied it will prove the new Mass is invalid. He has simply provided for his readers the conclusion that he believes one will arrive at if, according to Fr. Trinchard, he is honest and when one actually applies the principle to the new Mass.

Dear reader, this is no argument. It is simply providing a conclusion WITHOUT substantiation, at least at this point in the book. Not only that, Fr. Trinchard does not even apply the principle to the new Mass. He goes on presuming the principle has actually been applied by him to the new Mass AND that he has proven that its application does in fact prove the new Mass to be invalid. But he does neither at this point in the book. It is not until three chapters later when he applies the principle to the consecration prayers of the new Mass (Chapter 12, "Comparing Consecration," p. 179ff). But here he bases his conclusions upon the unproven presumption that the words of the new form *necessarily* have a meaning different from the "canonized liturgy." But his definitions do not have this necessity. Thus, his conclusions cannot be sustained since they lack necessity of meaning, as they depend upon the two erroneous presumptions listed back on page 41 (top).

Fr. Trinchard (p.182 and elsewhere) and others accuse those who say the new Mass with, among other things, the sin of omission. They base this on the fact that if one is to omit words from the sacramental form, one commits the sin of omission. Now, this is true concerning the words belonging to each particular Rite. But is this accusation applicable to those who say the new Mass? No. The sin of omission is not involved here because this is a new order of Mass (Novus Order Missae), a new rite of Mass. The words of the Tridentine Rite Mass have not been changed or omitted, they are the same as they have always been -*in the Tridentine Rite*. Just as the sacramental form is different in other Rites, so is the sacramental form different in the Novus Ordo Rite, for it is a new rite (see below). A priest is guilty of the sin of omission only in ommitting the words which belong to the sacramental form of that particular rite with which he is using.

On pages 184-185, Fr. Trinchard interprets the use of "IT" in the new form whereby "the bread being Christ" thus implies that the bread is not destroyed to make present the body of Christ (p. 184). But this is not necessitated by the use of "it." This is so precisely because "it" (the bread) does not become Christ's sacred Body until after the words, "this is my body," are pronounced. Thus, the use of "it" *before* that point is entirely consistent with what is occurring. Yes, one may interpret this heretically, but the words do not necessitate such an interpretation. (Fr. James Wathen makes the same argument on pages 89-90 in "The Great Sacrilege") If Fr. Trinchard wants to stay consistent, then he should uphold the very principle he claims to be employing from "The Abbot" (Abbot Gasquet) in reference to the Anglican Ordinal:

> "The new form carefully and systematically excluded every word
> that could be interpreted to mean that the candidate was ordained
> to be a sacrificing priest."

The principle here is that to exclude every word that COULD be interpreted to mean that which the Church teaches and intends is to render the sacrament null and void. However, the new form does NOT "exclude every word that could be interpreted to mean" that which the Church teaches and intends. Fr. Trinchard has no argument against validity on this point because his argument and the interpretation upon which it rests lacks necessity, the necessity of an heretical meaning.

We also know the use and placement of the word "it" in the N.O.M. does not necessitate a heretical meaning as Fr. Trinchard thinks it implies because in some of the Eastern Rites the word "it" (in reference to the pre-consecrated bread) is used right up to the words of the Consecration of the bread.

1. Chaldean (or East Syrian) Rite (in union with Rome), Anaphora of the Apostles (Sts. Addai & Maris): "… taking bread, He blessed IT, and broke IT, gave IT to His disciples and said: take, eat, this is my body…"

2. An ancient form of the Liturgy of St. Mark (Alexandrian Rite) says: "… He took bread into his holy hands, gave thanks, blessed IT, broke IT and gave IT to his disciples and apostles saying: take, and all of you eat IT: this is my body…"

The word "it" in each of these formulas *could* be understood to be referencing the pre-consecrated bread, however such an understanding is not necessitated. Also, since the validity of these other rites have never been questioned, it means that the use of the word "it" at these points does not necessitate a heretical meaning. Nevertheless, as Michael Davies pointed out in "Pope Paul's New Mass" (The Angelus Press, 1980) "this ambiguity does not occur in the Latin version where '*hoc*" which is neuter and singular, must refer to '*Corpus*' which is also singular." And since we are required to understand translations of sacramental forms only "in accordance with the mind of the Church as expressed in the original Latin text," the objection is thus answered. Therefore, Fr. Paul Trinchard's (and Fr. Wathen's) arguments and position on this point can not be maintained.

As just proven earlier in this section, because the words "for all" do not necessitate those meanings which would change the signification of the purpose/end for which the Mass was instituted, the new form does not make the Consecration/Mass invalid. Therefore we can trust that the new Mass is valid (provided that it is done with the other conditions being met for validity). Thus there is no change in signification from "for many" to "for all" which "clearly determines the predicate." That neither heretical meanings nor different significations are necessitated by the text means that doubt of validity is not necessitated. Therefore, no individual has the cause, let alone the right, to cause others to doubt the validity of the N.O.M. One who does doubt is in fact disobeying the Church which demands that the faithful understand what she approves "according to the ancient and continual faith of the universal Church" (Vatican I).

OBJECTION II: But does not the lack of explicitness in reference to a propitiatory sacrifice in the offertory of the new Mass indicate that the intent is different from what the Church traditional teaches?

ANSWER: No, not necessarily. This is one of Fr. Trinchard's attempted "proofs" against the validity of the N.O.M. Because certain offertory prayers lack explicitness concerning a propitiatory sacrifice does not mean that the intent has change. For if the priest intends to do what it is the Church does with this act, then he fulfills the necessary requirement of intention. You see, all that is involved in what it is the Church does (and what she teaches what she is doing here and what the holy Sacrifice is about) does not have to be explicitly contained in the actual offertory prayers or the canon. The offertory prayers and the Canon are not primarily didactic in their purpose. The Church's infallible teaching already provides for us what it is the Church does at this moment. If this were not the case, then the entire theology/doctrinal teaching of the Church concerning the Holy Eucharist and the Holy Sacrifice of the Mass would have to be contained in the offertory prayers and the Canon of the Mass. But not even the Traditional Roman Canon, nor any of the eastern Rite Canons, accomplishes such. Therefore, a lack of explicitness does not indicate a lack of proper intention. This is another reason why proper catechizing should been done.

Now, "*although the Mass contains much instruction for the faithful,*" as the Church declared at Trent, it does not mean that the entire theology of the Mass is contained therein. In fact, because the theology and teaching of the Church concerning the Mass are not entirely present even in the traditional offertory prayers and the Canon, the Fathers at Trent decreed, in Session XXII: "The Doctrine of the Most Holy Sacrifice of the Mass" (Chapter 8), that pastors are to *"explain some of the things which are read at Masses,... and expound some mystery of this most holy sacrifice, especially on Sundays and feast days"* (Denz. 946). Pastors must do this, because the entire teaching of the Church on the Holy Sacrifice is not expounded upon or declared in the prayers of the Mass. The Mass is primarily a prayer and offering to God, not an instructional course. This is why the faithful do not even need to hear the prayers of the priest.

OBJECTION III: The words "for all" can not signify the grace effected by the Sacrament (union of the faithful with the Mystical Body of Christ), because the Church teaches that it is the words "for many" which signify the effect. The Dimond Brothers have proven this.

ANSWER: We know this is not true not only because some Eastern Rite forms have used "for all," and these properly signified the effect of the Sacrament, but also because the words of the new form do not necessitate a meaning contrary to Catholic teaching, by which teaching we must understand what the new form signifies. The Dimond brothers have an article on their web page entitled: *"Short, Irrefutable and Devastating proof from a new angle that the word 'all' in place of 'many' renders the New Mass invalid."* Let us look at what they present on this point.

Peter Dimond:

> *Since the union of the faithful with Christ/the Mystical Body is the grace effected by the Sacrament of the Eucharist* – or what is also called the reality of the Sacrament (*Res Sacramenti*) or the grace proper to the Sacrament of the Eucharist– this grace must be signified in the Form of the Consecration for it to be valid, as Pope Leo XIII teaches.

> Pope Leo XIII, *Apostolicae Curae*, 1896:"All know that **the Sacraments of the New Law**, as sensible and efficient signs of invisible grace, **must both signify the grace which they effect and effect the grace which they signify."**

Pope Leo XIII, *Apostolicae Curae*, 1896: "**That form cannot be considered apt or sufficient for a Sacrament which omits that which it must essentially signify.**"

Pope Eugene IV, Council of Florence,: "…**this [the traditional form] is a fitting way to signify the effect of this sacrament, that is, the union of the Christian people with Christ.**"

Okay, so we must look at the Traditional Form of Consecration and find where this grace – the union of the faithful with Christ – is signified.

[So far, so good. Now, after demonstrating how the words previous to "for you and for many" in the consecration formula do not signify the effect of the Sacrament, i.e., the union of the faithful with the Mystical Body of Christ, Dimond finally comes to the crucial phrase.]

The words "for you and for many" denote **the members** of the Mystical Body who have received such remission [of sins].

Thus, we can see that the words "FOR YOU AND FOR MANY UNTO THE REMISSION OF SINS" are the words in the Form of Consecration which signify the union of the faithful with Christ/the union of the Mystical Body of Christ – which is the grace proper to the Sacrament of the Eucharist.

Now, if we look to the Novus Ordo Form of Consecration, do we find the Mystical Body/the union of the faithful with Christ [the grace proper to the Sacrament of the Eucharist] signified? Remember, the Form must signify the Mystical Body in order for it to be valid. Here is the form of Consecration in the New Mass or Novus Ordo:

"This is my body. This is the cup of my blood, of the new and eternal testament. It shall be shed for you and for all so that sins may be forgiven."

Is the union of the Mystical Body of Jesus Christ signified by the words "for you and for all so that sins may be forgiven"? No. Are all men part of the Mystical Body? No. Are all men part of the faithful united with Christ? No. We can see very clearly that the New Mass or Novus Ordo most certainly does not signify the union of the Mystical Body [the grace proper to the Sacrament of the Eucharist], and therefore it is not a valid sacrament!

One does not have to say anything more… the New Mass is not valid! [End quote]

Dimond's conclusion does not follow. You should notice with the above questions that Peter Dimond has actually changed the question. The question is not whether all men are part of the Mystical Body of Christ or make up the faithful united with Christ. We know dogmatically that this will never be. However, he has made a misleading shift here. The question, nay, the ENTIRE issue here, is whether or not the WORDS "for all" of the new sacramental form necessitate the universally inclusive meaning/sense of all men of all time being united to Christ in His Mystical Body. As demonstrated above, logically they do not necessitate such an erroneous meaning. Hence, there is no change in signification. Therefore, the New Mass most certainly does correctly signify the grace proper to the Sacrament, which is the union of ALL the faithful (not just some or many of them) upon whom the Blood (or grace) of Christ is efficacious with the Mystical Body of Christ. Thus, the Dimond article fails to prove that the New Mass is invalid. (We will see later on that Patrick Omlor also changes the question.)

OBJECTION IV: It is clear that those who composed the N.O.M. and who translated it were Liberals intent on undermining Catholic teaching. The new Mass is a result of their heretical views and intentions, thus it cannot be valid.

ANSWER: In terms of the last sentence, this is not true at all. The so-called authors of the new Mass do not (and cannot) determine CHURCH teaching concerning sacramental forms. Their intent has no bearing on the words themselves. (If they did intend to destroy the validity of the Mass, well, they failed because, as we have demonstrated above, the words "for all" do not necessitate a heretical meaning, nor do they fail to signify properly.) Once the Vicar of Christ approved and authorized its promulgation, then, of necessity, it demands to be understood according to Church teaching as demanded at Vatican I. In fact, we have NO RIGHT to interpret the new form in ANY other way than according to what the Church teaches concerning the Holy Sacrifice of the Mass. Thus, just because Liberals and Modernists, sedevecantists and even some traditionalists, interpret the new sacramental form in an heretical way, does not mean that the new form therefore objectively signifies and means such. It only means that those who do so are mistaken. As mentioned before, there is nothing in the words themselves of the new sacramental form which prohibit one from understanding them in an orthodox way, and thus in accord with Church teaching on the Holy Sacrifice of the Mass. Put simply: there is nothing in the new form which denies proper signification.

As mentioned before, the Sacred Congregation for the Doctrine of the Faith declared: that [the translations of the new form] *must be understood in accordance with the mind of the Church as expressed in the original Latin text.*

Therefore, *it is what the Church means by these words which is the determining factor*; NOT what certain individuals may subjectively think.

Think of it this way: just because Liberals and Modernists interpret in a heretical way numerous Catholic dogmas does not mean that the words of a defined dogma actually mean what the Liberals think or want them to mean. It is how the Church understands and uses the dogmatic formulas that matters. This very same principle applies to the new sacramental form of the N.O.M.

As previously mentioned, what matters is that if the Catholic Church pronounces that a particular sacramental rite is a sufficient and proper means for conferring a particular sacrament (as she has for the N.O.M. See Part VI), then it is valid, and the faithful must accept it. The Church's judgment is not dependant upon, nor influenced in any way upon the intentions of those who composed the rite, and the Church has declared that the new forms of the Eucharistic prayers do confect the sacrament. The fact to be learned here is that the Church's authority and how it is exercised is not affected by the intentions of individual men. This, then, leads us to look at Papal authority in relation to the Sacraments in general and the offering of the Holy Sacrifice of the Mass in particular.

POINT IV:

PAPAL AUTHORITY

Another related question concerning the New Mass and its validity is whether or not the Pope has the authority to modify an existing rite, or even promulgate a new Rite of Mass. Also, can a Pope change the language of the Sacred Liturgy? If one Pope solemnly forbids any changes in a certain Rite, as Pope St. Pius V declared with *Quo Primum*, does this mean that no changes at all can be made to that Rite by future pontiffs; or that no new rites can be promulgated? Also, implicit in the position of those who doubt or deny the validity of the N.O.M. is this question: can the Pope authorize an invalid liturgy?

Let us deal with these questions in their opposite order. Can the Roman Pontiff authorize an invalid liturgy? One cannot conceive that the Pope could authorize an invalid Mass worldwide without the gates of Hell having prevailed against us. And we know, infallibly, that *that* cannot take place (Mat.28:20; Jn.14:16). Guarding the Sacred Liturgy is part of the duty of the Church. Pope Pius XI made it clear in the Apostolic Constitution, *Divini Cultus* (20 December, 1928):

> The Church has received from Christ her founder the charge of safe-guarding divine worship. It is therefore her duty, while protecting the essence of the Holy Sacrifice and of the sacraments, to prescribe whatever will best control that august and public ministry - ceremonies, rites, texts, prayers, chant - which is properly called liturgy, or sacred action par excellence.

If the Church, in promulgating the N.O.M., has failed in her duty to safeguard divine worship, then the Church has defected from an essential part of her mission. But the Church is indefectible, therefore the N.O.M. is not invalid. If the Church, in the most universally used rite for the last 30 years, is leading the vast majority of her members to hell by the use of a sacrilegious rite, then the gates of hell HAVE prevailed over the Church, for the Church in her essential role of sanctifying IS visible in the celebration of the Sacraments. In fact, she is most visible in the celebration of her Sacramental Rites. As Pope Pius XII declared: "The Church is visible in her life, in her worship, in her sacraments, in her hierarchy" (Allocution of February 17, 1942).

1. QUO PRIMUM

OBJECTION I: Does not the papal bull *Quo Primum*(1570) bind the successors of Pope St. Pius V? After reading the solemn decrees of the Bull, it certainly seems like it does.

ANSWER: *Quo Primum* does not bind any of the successors of St. Peter, for no pope has an authority higher than another pope. *Quo Primum* is a disciplinary decree, and then, only applicable to the Western Rite church; it had (has) no binding power on the Eastern Rite churches which are exempted. So how could subsequent Vicars of Christ themselves be bound to it when Eastern Rite bishops and even "lowly" Eastern Rite priests were (are) not bound to it? A misunderstanding of the very nature of authority, particularly Papal authority, is at work here for those who think *Quo Primum* could bind future Pontiffs.

QUESTION: Did any predecessors and/or successors of Pius V use this type of decree and language before in regards to liturgy?

ANSWER: Yes, and yet these binding decrees with the use of full apostolic authority were not understood as binding upon future pontiffs by those pontiffs who over-turned them.

EXAMPLE A: MASS IN SLAVONIC

1. Pope Adrian II (867-72), in his Decree ordaining the use of Slavonic declared:

> "Let all those be cast forth from the fold who condemn this use of the vernacular."

This statement is as strong as it can get since it threatens excommunication. This decree is contained in the *"Regeta Pontificum Romanorum,"* and we see that the Roman Pontiff is making it clear that anyone who rejects what it states would be "cast forth from the fold" (i.e. the Church). Would this not also apply to future pontiffs? It was stated without any qualifications. Well, future pontiffs did not think nor act as if it did apply to them.

2. In the year 873 and again in 879, the very next Pope, John VIII, drafted two decrees forbidding any use whatsoever of the Slavonic vernacular in the Holy Sacrifice of the Mass! Thus he contradicted what the previous pope had decreed with a threat of excommunication. (These decrees can be found in the *Patrologia cursus completus* of J. P. Migne, no. 126.)

Now two questions people ask of Pope Paul VI should also be asked of Pope John VIII, here: 1) Did Pope John VIII have the authority to change a Papal decree which threatened excommunication if said decree was denied? Yes, he did. 2) Did not Pope John VIII incur the excommunication decreed by Pope Adrian in suppressing the vernacular? No, he did not. No pope can bind another pope in matters of discipline. This is so even if said discipline is meant to be a means of safeguarding doctrine/ revelation (for it may not be the *only* means).

3. Yet, the very next year with his encyclical *"Ad Svatapluk"* (June 13, 880), Pope John VIII himself did an abrupt about-face and solemnly approved of the Slavonic Mass in the vernacular. He changed his own former decree which forbade the use of the Slavonic vernacular.

4. Then, his successor, Pope Stephen VI (885-891), in his full and supreme authority as Pope, condemned and forbade the use of Slavonic in the Mass "under pain of excommunication" (*Patrologia*, no. 129). So now we have the next pontiff solemnly condemning the use of Slavonic and thus contradicting his predecessor's command.

So far we have three popes officially damning and counter-damning: those who do and those who don't. Confused yet? Well, read on.

5. But to make matters worse for the Slavs, Pope Alexander II (1061-73), at the Council of Salada, decreed using his full authority and "in perpetuity" that the Mass could NEVER again be recited in Slavonic, but only in Greek or Latin. (This decree and council can be found in *Rerum Liturgicarum*, no. 1, Sec. 9.) This is the same forcefulness used in *Quo Primum*: "in perpetuity" and "never again" to be used.

6. Surely the final termination of Masses in Slavonic seemed assured and complete when Pope St. Gregory VII (1073-85), in his solemn and full authority prohibited the use of the Slavonic language in Holy Mass "under ANY circumstance" (*Pontifical Register*, no. 5151).

It appears that these last two decrees have settled the matter. We have being "cast forth from the fold," "in perpetuity," "never again" to be allowed, and its disallowance "under any circumstance" working against future Pontiffs. But is this the case? No!

7. YET, two centuries later, Pope Innocent IV (1243-54), by virtue of his apostolic authority, countermanded every single one of his predecessors who forbade it and reinstates the legitimate use of the Slavonic vernacular in the Sacred Liturgy. (*Annuario D' Ecclesia*, 1248).

8. Pope Leo XIII assured this continuation of the Slavonic Mass in the year 1880 with his Decree Grande Munis; and finally Pope St. Pius X canonized the legitimacy of the Slavonic vernacular on December 18, 1906 (*Decreta Authentica*, no. 4063).

EXAMPLE B: VERNACULAR TRANSLATIONS

1. Pope Alexander VII (1655-67), in response to the attempted publication of a French-Latin Missal, declared in his authoritative Bull, *Ad Aures Nostras* (1660): "We therefore by special act and from certain knowledge condemn, disapprove and prohibit FOR ALL TIME and will regard as condemned, disapproved and prohibited the above-mentioned missal –no matter where and under what conditions it may in the future by written or published, and to the faithful of whatever rank, order, state of life, dignity, honor or pre-eminence, under pain of excommunication

(*latae sententiae*) to be incurred by the vigor of the law itself, WE FOREVER FORBID its printing, reading and possession."

2. In 1778, Pope Pius VI, in the Bull, *Auctorum Fidei*, condemned the simplification of rites, the use of the vernacular language in the Mass, and the praying of the Canon aloud.

3. On June 6, 1857, by authority of Blessed Pope Pius IX, a decree was promulgated which declared: "It is not permitted to translate the ordinary of the Mass into the Vernacular and print the same for use of the faithful, nor can such a work get the approval of a bishop."

It again appears that the matter of vernacular translations was settled once and for all. It was "condemned for all time" and "forever forbidden."

4. YET, in 1877, Pope Pius IX began to allow local bishops to approve layman's missals, and Pope St. Pius X allowed vernacular translations and usage on a universal level. Thus the terminology of prohibiting "for all time" and "forever forbidding" was not understood by Pius X as binding upon him.

What can we learn from all these counter decrees and condemnations? We see that, despite the use of the full authority of the Papal office/powers binding something in matters of discipline, even using the most forceful of terms such as "in perpetuity," or "for all time," or "forever forbidden," a future pope can still unbind these very same decrees. Popes cannot bind future pope in matters of discipline, and all that is involved in liturgical rites belongs to the realm of discipline. *Quo Primum* was not dealing with dogma, per se. St. Pius V makes it clear that he is dealing with the Missal itself (not the doctrine/ theology of Holy Mass) and:

> "that priests may know which prayers to use, and which rites and ceremonies they were required to observe in the celebration of Masses." (see end of second, or third paragraph -depending on edition)

A document that deals with the prayers, ceremonies and rites of the Holy Mass belongs, by definition, to the realm of discipline, not dogma. Of course ceremonies/rites are to reflect and embody doctrine, and often contain non-dogmatic expressions of the doctrines upon which they reflect. St. Pius was rightly concerned with safeguarding such. But he never said or implied that only one set of prayers, ceremonies, and thus only *one* rite, could safeguard the doctrines contained in the Holy Mass; otherwise, every other rite (both eastern and western) would have been abrogated, but they were not. Thus, Pope Paul VI was not bound by *Quo Primum* but had the authority to either revise the missal of St. Pius V, or even to introduce and approve a new rite. (We deal with this authority to do either below.) He was well aware that *Quo Primum* had no authority over him when he decreed: "We decree that these laws and prescriptions be firm and effective now and in the future, notwithstanding, to the extent necessary, the apostolic constitutions and ordinances issued by our predecessors and other prescriptions, even those deserving particular mention and amendment" (*Missale Romanum*, 3 April 1969).

NEVERTHELESS:

One might say, "Quo Primum was a Papal Bull; and Papal Bulls are of the highest exercise of Papal authority." Well, ideally speaking this may be so, but not in actuality. Papal authority can be exercised with whatever documentary means the pope chooses. For example:

Pope St. Pius V himself (yes, the *Quo Primum* pope) confirmed and ratified the constitution of the Society of Jesus with two separate Bulls. In fact, there were a total of ten Bulls issued confirming the Society. Yet in the year 1773, the Society of Jesus was total abolished by a Papal Brief; a mere Papal Brief! Not a Bull, not a Decree, not a Papal Constitution or Apostolic Letter was used. This was the "Brief of Suppression" issued by Pope Clement XIV in the year 1773. This one little Brief alone wiped out two whole Bulls of Pope St. Pius V and *eight* other Bulls of Sovereign Pontiffs by a single stroke of the pen. (Whether or not one thinks this Brief was just is not material to the present matter.) And the Popes, whether correct or not, whether exercising the greatest prudence or not, must be obeyed in matters of discipline, unless said discipline necessarily undermines the faith.

This very same principle applies to *Quo Primum*. Actually, those who argue Pope St. Pius V's Quo Primum against Pope Paul VI's action are arguing apples and oranges (heck, it may even be apples and a non-fruit: peas?) Pope Paul VI didn't make ANY changes to the Tridentine Rite and this is what St. Pius V was forbidding; we still have the traditional Latin Rite Mass (I assist at one every Sunday). Rather, Paul VI promulgated a new order of Mass, a new Rite, and *Quo Primum* does not explicitly forbid this. However, even if *Quo Primum* did forbid this, the above facts concerning the nature and exercise of Papal authority prove that *Quo Primum* can not be binding upon a future Vicar of Christ. Otherwise, the very title "Vicar of Christ" as applied to each Roman Pontiff is quite obsolete. Quo Primum only forbids changes to the traditional Latin/Roman Rite, but it does not forbid the promulgation of any new rites. We must not read more into the text than is there. Remember, St. Pius V's authority is no greater than any other Pope's.

One last question: Did Pope Paul VI have the authority to introduce, approve and promulgate a new Rite of Mass? Yes, he did. Pope Pius XII made this clear when he stated in *Mediator Dei* (November 20, 1947) that:

> "the Sovereign Pontiff alone enjoys the right to recognize and establish any practice touching the worship of God, to introduce and approve new rites, as also to modify those he judges to require modification." (# 58)

Earlier the Sovereign Pontiff stated:

> From time immemorial the ecclesiastical hierarchy has exercised this right in matters liturgical. It has organized and regulated divine worship, enriching it constantly with new splendor and beauty, to the glory of God and the spiritual profit of Christians. What is more, it has not been slow--keeping the substance of the Mass and sacraments carefully intact--to modify what it deemed not altogether fitting, and to add what appeared more likely to increase the honor paid to Jesus Christ and the august Trinity, and to instruct and stimulate the Christian people to greater advantage. (# 49)

Thus Pope Paul VI was exercising his proper authority when introducing and approving a new rite, or "modifying those he judged to require modification." The old Canon Law (1918), which was in effect when he promulgated the new rite, also recognized this right (cf. Code of Canon Law, can. 1257, 1261). Traditionalists may not like the change; and we may disagree as to its wisdom, since it breaks with tradition. However, we cannot reject the authority of Pope Paul VI to do such. By the very nature of Papal authority, *Quo Primum* cannot bind any future pope, nor nullify the use of papal authority over the Sacred Liturgy. This is quite different from attempting to change the substance of the sacraments, which of course no pope can do that since the very substance of the sacraments come from Christ Himself.

Can a Pope change the language of the Sacred Liturgy? The original language of the Holy Sacrifice of the Mass was Aramaic. It was immediately offered after the Last Supper in both Aramaic and Hebrew. Tradition gives witness to the fact that when St. Peter established the papacy in Rome in the year 42, he then began to offer the Mass in the Greek language. He instituted the change of liturgical language from Aramaic or Hebrew because in Rome, the center of the whole civilized world at that time, Greek was the spoken vernacular. He even required St. Mark, his scribe and interpreter, to draft his Gospel in Greek under his personal direction. But by the middle of the 4th century, Latin had replaced Greek as the spoken tongue of the entire Empire. Therefore, in the year 382, Pope St. Damasus changed the Mass again and put it into Latin for the people. Actually, it might well have been Pope St. Victor, some 200 years before St. Damasus, who gets credit for being the first pontiff to say the Mass in the language of the Romans; but it was Pope St. Damasus who officially gave the Latin Mass as such to the Universal Church, just as he ordered St. Jerome to translate the entirety of the Bible from Hebrew and Greek into Latin.

There were several other languages used in saying the Mass which the Church traditionally allowed. Traditionally there are five major Rites and twenty-five sub-rites subject to the Pope of Rome; and among these, a total of nine different languages and various dialects have been used, with at least one of them - Rumanian - having always been a living vernacular.

These historical facts, and those just listed concerning the use of Slavonic in the Mass, prove that the Roman Pontiff, having supreme jurisdiction on earth, has the right to put the Mass into any language which he choose to be convenient to men and conducive to the honor and glory of God. However, Mass in the vernacular has traditionally prevailed as a compromise, and is now the norm for the West, but this in no way brings into question its licitness or the Pontiff's authority to allow such.

2. SACRED SCRIPTURE

A parallel example concerning the official edition of the Latin Vulgate can be used to help us better understand this issue of Papal authority. The Council of Trent had called for an officially sponsored critical edition of the Latin Vulgate [April 8, 1546]. Serious work was undertaken over the next forty years, and the so called "Sixtine Vulgate" of 1590 was finally issued. The same type of language used by Pope St. Pius V in *Quo Primum* was used by Pope Sixtus V (1585-90) when he declared that the 1590 version/edition of the Vulgate was FOREVER valid. Yet, because of errors, it had to be revised and reissued in the so-called Sixto-Clementine Text of 1592-98. Finally, the Clementine text [under Pope Clement VIII] of 1612 became the official catholic text, and was reissued as late as 1959.

Pope Sixtus V was in fact a highly accomplished man, but he was too eager to get the revised Vulgate published. As a result of his personal efforts the Vulgate edition of 1590 was riddled with errors. Nevertheless, Pope Sixtus then set forth the results of his work as not only official but also forever unalterable. The mistake was realized afterwards and his embarrassed successor, Clement VIII, had to make an effort to recover as many copies as possible. In all, over three thousand errors had to be corrected! Thus, despite the fact that Pope Sixtus VI declared a version of the Bible as "official and forever unalterable," a succeeding Pontiff did change it within two years. The language of Sixtus VI appeared as solemn and just as perpetually binding as the language used by pope St. Pius V in *Quo Primum*, yet this was not binding upon a future Pontiff, for just like a rite, or the revisions within a rite, the particular edition of Sacred Scripture falls under Ecclesiastical discipline.

3. COUNCIL OF FLORENCE

OBJECTION II: It should not be forgotten that the sacramental form for the Latin/Roman Rite has already been dogmatically defined on at the Council of Florence in 1441. This fact should have made any of the aforementioned unnecessary. The argument is really grounded in authority, and the N.O.M. departs from this infallible definition.

ANSWER: This is a misuse of the term "dogmatic definition," for this term automatically means that it is UNIVERSALLY applicable to all Catholics of every rite, universally binding on all Catholics, and FORMALLY revealed by God as dogma. But the declaration from Florence of which you speak does not claim such, nor was it universally applicable to the entire Church. To think it does is either the result of sloppy reading, or a misunderstanding of the nature of a dogmatic definition. It only stated at Florence that, "the [Roman] Church uses this form of the words…" (therein states the traditional formula; Denz. 715). Yes, this is an infallible statement, but it is simply declaring what sacramental form the Latin/Roman Rite Church uses. In other words, it is only stating as a matter of fact what the Roman Church uses in its particular rite. It is not forbidding anything, nor denying the validity of the Sacramental forms of other Catholic Rites. This is not in any way a dogmatic definition which declares that God has revealed one and only one sacramental form. Thus, this statement from Florence is not declaring that a new rite, or new form could never be approved. Since the N. O. Rite is a new order of Mass, this declaration does not apply to it, just as it does not apply to other Catholic rites.

4. COUNCIL OF TRENT

Advocates of the position of Mr. Omlor, et al, often use the following Canon from the Seventh Session of the Council of Trent (March 3, 1547) against the promulgation of the N.O.M. The canon states:

> "If anyone says that the received and approved rites of the Catholic Church, accustomed to be used in the administration of the sacraments, may be despised or omitted by the ministers without

sin and at their pleasure, or may be changed by any pastor of the churches to other new ones, let him be anathema."(Canon 13)

We ask: Does the promulgation of and/or the saying of the N.O. Mass come under this condemnation? No, not necessarily, unless the priest who says the N.O. in fact has the attitude of despising the received and approved Rites, and omits those things belonging to *that individual Rite* at his pleasure, or changes an approved Rite to another new one. But the N.O.M. is an approved Rite, so simply saying the new rite (which has papal approval) does not qualify one as coming under this anathema, unless the priest omits or changes that which is approved from the N.O. Rite itself (or any other Rite). If anything, those who are performing a hybrid of rites come under the strong arm of this canon (and there are some priests doing this).

Now, there are some who have declared that Pope Paul VI comes under the part of Canon 13 which states that those who say "that the received and approved rites of the Catholic Church... may be changed by any pastor of the churches to other new ones, let him be anathema."

Does the Pope fall under the "any pastor" condition? No, he does not. And this for two reasons:

1. Pope Paul VI made absolutely no changes to the actual Tridentine Rite itself. In other words, he did not change the traditional Latin/Roman Rite to a new one. He simple promulgated a new order of Mass (or a new rite) which is loosely based upon the Traditional Latin/Roman Rite; but he left the traditional Rite completely alone; and the condition stated by the canon condemns those who hold that the received Rite can "be changed... to other new ones." But the *received* rite was not changed, just a new rite was added. You see? The condition for which the anathema applies is not even achieved here. The Traditional Latin/Roman Rite was not changed to a new one, we still have it.

2. No disciplinary document can be binding on a subsequent Roman Pontiff as just demonstrated (# 1 above: Quo Primum). If anyone still does not recognize this, then he actually has a more fundamental confusion concerning Papal authority, its nature, its limits, is function, etc.

Now, we know the substance of the sacraments cannot be changed or even touched as Pope Leo XIII declared in his Bull *Apostolicae Curae* (1896). However, as already seen, the establishment and approval of new rites does belong to the Church, and this would include those sacramental forms belonging to particular rites, so long as the substance is not changed. The Council of Trent (Session 21, Chapter 2), declared concerning "the power of the Church as regards the dispensation of the Sacraments of the Eucharist"(Session 21, Chapter 2):

"It furthermore declares, that this power has ever been in the Church, that, in the dispensation of the sacraments, their substance being untouched, it may ordain,- or change, what things soever it may judge most expedient, for the profit of those who receive, or for the veneration of the said sacraments, according to the difference of circumstances, times, and places.... Wherefore, holy Mother Church, knowing this her authority in the administration of the sacraments, although the use of both species has,- from the beginning of the Christian religion, not been infrequent, yet, in progress of time, that custom having been already very widely changed,- she, induced by weighty and just reasons,- has approved of this custom of communicating under one species, and decreed that it was to be held as a law; which it is not lawful to reprobate, or to change at pleasure, without the authority of the Church itself."

The Church does have the authority to set and prescribe the form and matter of the sacraments, where Our Lord has not done so already. The Church does have the authority to prescribe the "matter" of the Holy Eucharist, and has exercised this authority: leavened bread for the Eastern Rites and unleavened bread for the West. The Church has even prescribed and approved different forms for the Sacrament, for most of the Eastern Rite liturgies do not have the words, "mystery of faith," in their forms for consecration, nor are any of their forms exactly the same (see Appendix below).

Neither of these approved variations are trivial differences as far as form and matter are concerned, yet neither of these have touched upon the substance of the Sacrament (i.e., that which makes it what it is, and without which the Sacrament would not be). The substance is still the same despite these Church-approved differences in both the form and matter of the Sacrament. And as has been demonstrated in this work, the substance of this Sacrament has not been touched with the addition of the new consecration form for the new Mass. As infallibly declared at Trent, the Church has the lawful authority to do what she has done with the new Mass.

*(In regard to the point above: When a large group of Jacobites came back and joined Rome in 1781, and became known as Catholic Syrians, their rite, the Rite of St. James translated into Syrian, was examined, and revised by Rome. Of the over 50 Anaphoras, most were deleted and only seven were retained. Here we have Rome deleting numerous Anaphoras which had many centuries of use and previous approval. The authority of Rome to do such editing and revising has never been questioned.)

A New Rite or a Revision of the Old Rite?

Is the N.O.M. a new rite (i.e. a new order of Mass), or is it only a revision of the old rite? If it is not a new rite, but only a revision of the old rite, then does this not come under the solemn prohibition of Pope St. Pius V in Quo Primum? The answer to this is, no. It has just been proven that *Quo Primum* does not bind future pontiffs, despite its authoritative language. It has also been proven that the pope has the proper authority to revise old rites, or establish or approve new rites. As Pope Pius XII affirmed in *Mediator Dei*:

> "the Sovereign Pontiff alone enjoys the right to recognize and establish any practice touching the worship of God, to introduce and approve new rites, as also to modify those he judges to require modification." (# 58)

Pope Paul VI had the authority to recognize and establish ANY practice touching the worship of God, *to introduce and approve new rites*, so long as the substance of the sacrament is not changed; and it has been proven in this work that the substance of the Blessed Sacrament has not been changed in the N.O.M. At the same time, even if the N.O.M. is only a revision of the Rite of Mass codified by St. Pius V, the Sovereign Pontiff has the authority also to *modify* those rites he judges to require modification.

Let us look at the situation. There are a number of indications that the legislator of the N.O.M., Pope Paul VI, considered it a new rite (based on the old rite). Pope Paul VI himself called it a "new rite" two times in his Address introducing the new Mass to the faithful (17 March, 1969):

"[O]n the first Sunday of Advent, which falls on 30 November this year. That event is the introduction of a "NEW MASS RITE...""

"The unity between the Lord's Supper, the Sacrifice of the Cross, and the re-presentation of both in the Mass, is inviolably affirmed and celebrated in the NEW RITE, as it was in the old."

The N.O.M. is also called a "new rite" in the Instruction *Constitution Apostolica* (20 October, 1969; A.A.S. 61), which bears the title: "On gradually implementing the Apostolic Constitution Missale Romanum," which is the officially promulgated instruction concerning Pope Paul's Constitution. It states:

"The foregoing documents decreed that... the NEW RITE and the new text be used."

In the Notification "*Conferentia Episcopalium*" (28 October, 1974), it declares:

"Mass, whether in Latin or the vernacular, maybe celebrated lawfully only according to the RITE OF THE ROMAN MISSAL promulgated 3 April, 1969 by authority of Pope Paul VI."

Calling it simply the "Rite of the Roman Missal" presumes that it is a different, and therefore in this case a NEW, rite than that which was codified and promulgated by St. Pius V. Either way, whether the N.O.M. is actually a new rite within the Western portion of the Church, or only a modification/reform of an existing rite (viz. THE Roman Rite), the Sovereign Pontiff has the authority to approve and promulgate the N.O.M.

Some say that there has always been and should always be only one rite of Mass within the Latin Rite portion of the Church. But this is just plainly false. There are a number of rites within the Western or Latin portion of the Church. Some insist that these are merely sub-rites, not entirely different rites, but there are clear and explicit variations betweens these different rites. These rites include the Dominican Rite, Toledo Rite, Ambrosian/Milanese Rite, Carthusian Rite, Anglican Use Rite, Sarumite Rite (actually, the Sarum Use of the Latin/Roman Rite, a true sub-rite), as well as the traditional Roman (Tridentine) Rite. In fact, the Congregation for Divine Worship declared in its recent Instruction, *Redemptionis Sacramentum* (n.3), that there are "other Rites of the Latin Church that are duly acknowledged by law." (25 March, 2004). Therefore, one can only conclude that the N.O.M. is, in fact, a separate and distinct rite of Mass within the Latin Church.

Maybe Valid but…?

OBJECTION III: Some say that the N. O. M. still does not become acceptable should it be established that it contains no explicit heresy and that it is valid. As Cardinal Ottaviani warned, "The innovations in the Novus Ordo and the fact that all that is of perennial value finds only a minor place, if it subsists at all, could turn into a certainty the suspicion already prevalent, alas, in many circles, that truths which have always been believed by Christian people can be changed or ignored without infidelity to that sacred deposit of doctrine to which the Catholic faith is bound forever" (*The Ottaviani Intervention*, Tan Books and Publishers, pp.27-28).

ANSWER: If a Catholic knows his faith, the Catholic Faith, then he knows that nothing of the truths taught by the Church and received by the faithful can ever be changed. The doctrines which God has revealed and we believe are immutable. If a suspicion exists that "truths which have always been believed by Christian people can be changed or ignored without infidelity to that sacred deposit of doctrine to which the Catholic faith is bound forever" (as Cardinal Ottaviani declared), then that person who holds such suspicion, does not know or does not believe very strongly his Catholic Faith. Thus, the problem here is not inherent in the liturgy, but is the result of either poor catechesis, or it is the result of that particular person being slothful for not making the efforts to learn his faith properly. Thus, the problem, if such suspicion occurs, pre-exists in the person before he comes to the liturgy and thus the person is to blame, not the liturgy. Hence, as already noted: dogma/faith (and learning it/believing it) comes before liturgy.

OBJECTION IV: Some traditionalists hold that the N.O.M. can be said validly and that it is precisely because of this fact that sacrilege exists, since only that which is holy can be profaned, and mere bread and wine are not holy. So because of all that goes on within the N.O.M., and all that is omitted, is why sacrilege is committed.

ANSWER: It is true that only the sacred can be profaned, and thus for any sacrileges to be committed, the Sacred must be present in the first place. However, the objection offered is to be rejected on the basis of the following truth: The Holy Sacrifice of the Mass is offered on Three Levels:

• Christ to the Father;
• The Church (represented by the priest), the Body united with its Head, to the Blessed Trinity (through Him, in Him and with Him);
• The human participation in said sacrificial offering (external rites);

These levels are hierarchical in nature. Thus, the "value" of each is in accordance with its position within the hierarchical structure. Every Mass of every Rite involves all three levels. The first two are infinite in value. Thus, it is only on the last level where sacrilege can be committed. But that in nowise means that the Mass, as offered from the first two -and PRIMARY- levels ~ through Him, and with Him, and in Him ~ is sacrilegious. Catholics should know that there is a hierarchical order to everything. And the primary levels of offering the Holy Sacrifice of the Mass, the first and the second, outweigh infinitely the third level. The lowest level, with its lower value has no effect on the two higher levels. In other words, the higher levels are not subjected to the abuses of the lowest level -the human level.

Something else to remember is the very first Holy Sacrifice of the Precious Blood on altar of the Cross on Calvary. The "man part" there was atrociously sacrilegious and blasphemously sinful. But, 1) it was an infinitely honorable offering to God on the part of His Divine Son, and from which all sanctification and salvation come, AND 2) it was possible to attend it in good conscience, as did Our Lady and her companions, despite the attendant horrors.

The truth being defended here was also made clear by the Church at Trent, where, at the end of chapter 1, "On the Most Holy Sacrifice of the Mass," it was infallibly declared that the Mass:

> "…indeed, is that 'clean oblation' which cannot be defiled by *any* unworthiness or malice on the part of those who offer it." (Denz. 939; bold italics added)

This means that despite any abuse or unworthiness or malice which may be present at the N.O.M., the first two levels are still present. Therefore, contrary to those who accept its validity but consider it a sacrilege, the N.O.M. cannot be considered inherently sacrilegious or defiled simply because of the "man part" (third-lowest level) or those who offer it. Its sacrilegious aspects -if present- are limited exclusively to the "man part" and do not affect the first two levels of the offering. And no one is obligated to join in on this level when such scandalous aspects are present.

The following canon from the Council of Trent must also be considered: Canon 7 on the "Holy Sacrifice of the Mass" works against those who reject the N.O.M. altogether as an evil sacrilegious rite. It states:

> "If anyone says that the ceremonies, vestments, and outward signs, which the Catholic Church uses in the celebration of Masses, are incentives to impiety rather than the services of piety: let him be anathema."(Denz. 954)

The only way to get around this canon is to say that the Catholic Church did not promulgate this new rite, and thus does not use it (i.e. the Church is not present when this rite is performed), but that would mean at least three problems:

1. Any priest who offers the Holy Sacrifice with the new rite does so separated from union with the Church: (otherwise the Church IS there using this rite and thus canon 7 is in effect for those who say it is intrinsically evil);

2. Pope Benedict XVI (and John Paul II before him) offers the Holy Mass in this Rite, therefore he must be separated from the Church and is not the visible head of the Church; and

3. that Pope Paul VI, who promulgated the new rite, was not a real pope.

Therefore, the only way around this canon, as applied to the N.O.M., is to hold that the chair of Peter has been vacant since before Pope Paul VI was elected. In other words, the only way to avoid the canonical condemnation of Canon 7 on the Mass is to be a sedevecantist, and be correct in that position (i.e. the Chair of Peter really has been vacant since before Paul VI, who promulgated the N.O.M.). No one who acknowledges the legitimacy of the last three Roman Pontiffs can hold this position without being guilty of holding a position which is internally contradictory and thus refutes itself. However, as will be proven below, Pope Paul VI did properly and legally approve and promulgate the N.O.M. (see PART VI).

A Few Considerations

The Holy Eucharist, offered up in every Catholic Rite of the Mass, is at the same time both a sign and cause of unity as the Church teaches (Denz.875, 882); and the Vicar of Christ is the center of that unity, as the Church also teaches (Denz.1686, 1960). Yet, IF one rejects the very Rite of Mass which the Roman Pontiff not only approves, but also offers, THEN is he not in some way separating himself from Christ's Vicar, and thus from Christ? Is not this rejection of the very Rite offered by the Roman Pontiff, the center of unity and visible head of the Church on earth, at the least a schismatic attitude?

The Church infallible defined at Vatican I that the faithful are to be united to the Roman Pontiff and to submit to his authority in doctrinal matters of not only faith and morals, but "also be submissive to him in matters of liturgy and discipline." (Denz. 1831) Persons who today reject the New Mass and hold it as invalid are clearly disobeying the will and authority of the Holy Father and the mind of the Church. And it must be remembered, obedience to the Pope, in those areas where he has legitimate authority, and the liturgy is one of them, is obedience to Jesus Christ. It is a defined dogma of the Catholic Faith that: "it is absolutely necessary for the salvation of every human creature to be subject to the Roman Pontiff" (Pope Boniface VIII, Bull *Unam Sanctum*, 1302). Therefore, let no one consider himself free to reject the N.O.M. as invalid or intrinsically evil, or he separates himself from obedience to the Roman Pontiff, and thus from Christ Himself.

Is the New Mass of Pope Paul VI Invalid?

PART V:

Specific Refutations of Points Found in "The Robber Church"

Mr. Patrick H. Omlor spends much time giving background information in sacramental theology. Therefore, specific points on which this author shall critique do not appear until well into the body of his work. I will mark both the paragraph and page number of what I am addressing. Unfortunately, because of the large volume involved with this material, this critique will have to presume that the reader has a copy of *The Robber Church* in front of him to reference, or at least a copy of Mr. Omlor's work, "Questioning the Validity." Therefore, I will actually quote Mr. Omlor only a few times. I will also be making references to the four points from this present work established above as: Point I above, Point II above, etc. Any point made by Mr. Omlor that has no bearing on validity itself, will not be addressed. I warn the reader that there will be repetition in my comments and refutation because Mr. Omlor bases his different arguments and conclusions upon the same unproven and erroneous presumption concerning the words, "for all."

Questioning The Validity (pp. 16-81 in The Robber Church)

Paragraph # 21-30, pp. 26-27 (expounds upon the sacramental form for the traditional Roman Rite):

Of course this is the form, but only this exact form is necessary for the specific traditional Roman-Tridentine Rite. It does not apply to and thus is not required for other rites. We affirm, this exact form is essential for confecting the sacrament and thus for validity but, again, only in that rite to which it belongs, in Mr. Omlor's example it is the traditional Latin/Roman Rite. Therefore, because the N.O.M. does not use the specific form of the traditional Latin/Roman Rite does not mean that it does not confect the Sacrament, or that there is defect of form, since as a

NEW rite it has its own sacramental form. We know this assertion to be true because other valid rites do not use this exact form, yet their validity is not questioned. The N.O.M. is a new rite added to the Western portion of the Church, thus Mr. Omlor's conclusion does not apply.

 # 34-37, 39, p. 28 (declares if essential sense is changed, then the sacrament has been rendered invalid...):

Yes, the sacrament would be rendered invalid, but only IF it involves an essential change in signification. But Mr. Omlor must still establish that the new form in fact changes the essential meaning. Yet, Mr. Omlor fails to prove what he claims he shall show, and we have proven that no such change occurs.

 # 43-44, p. 29:

Mr. Omlor erroneously presumes that the form of the new rite is being used as a substitute for the old form of the traditional Latin/Roman Rite; but it is not a substitute. The New Form is simply the form belonging to the new rite. Thus, his conclusion does not follow.

 # 46, p. 29 (Omlor claims new form destroys "essential sense"):

So far the claim that the "new 'form' has destroyed the 'essential sense' of the words in the ancient, established form" is still unsubstantiated. Mr. Omlor now makes the claim but has yet to prove it. But he cannot do such as demonstrated in Points I-III.

 # 49, p. 30 (power of form derived *solely* from exact words of Christ):

Mr. Omlor is guilty of a slight-of-hand here, or he has misunderstood St. Thomas' point. Omlor states two points. He said: "the power of this sacrament is derived solely from the fact that the words spoken by the priest are the exact words of Our Lord" (emphasis by Omlor). First, the power does not come SOLELY from this, but comes from both the words spoken by Christ AND from the power of Holy Orders, otherwise, anyone can confect the Blessed Sacrament by repeating Our Lord's word. Second, no one actually speaks the exact words of Our Lord unless he pronounces them in Aramaic. Thus, to emphasize the word "exact" is misleading. What the vast majority of consecrations involve is a translation of Our Lord's words. Now, because having the same signification is what is at stake here, then if the translation is faithful to the meaning and signification of what Christ said, then no argument can be used against it. Also, if speaking the *exact* words of Christ were absolutely necessary to confect the Sacrament, then each and every Catholic Rite would have the exact same sacramental form for the consecration, but they do not. Thus, Mr. Omlor's specific point here cannot be maintained.

Mr. Omlor then proceeds to quote St. Thomas as if the Angelic Doctor was making the very same point that the power of the sacrament is derived solely from the fact that the words spoken by the priest are the *exact words* of Christ. But St. Thomas was not dealing with the point of the exactness of Christ's words (which is Mr. Omlor's argument here), but was only making the point that the priest "does nothing in perfecting this sacrament, except to pronounce the words of Christ" (ST, III, Q.78, Art. 1). As one can see, St. Thomas' point was not dealing with the issue of the necessity of the exactness of Christ's words as Omlor is dealing with, but simply with the nature of the action of the priest. This slight-of-hand by Mr. Omlor will mislead many who do not read carefully.

 # 51-53, p. 30 (words of Christ from tradition):

This point is dealt with below (p. 92) in "No Mystery of Faith: No Mass?"

 # 54, p. 30 (States that the form came from Christ, yet admits there has been editing of the rite of Mass down through history):

This argument here only substantiates the arguments in Point IV above: that a Pope has authority to edit and/or modify existing rites and promulgate new rites. In fact, in this example from Omlor we see that we have neither an apostle nor a Pope adding to (or editing) the form, but a "mere" bishop! (St. Basil, Bishop of Caesarea)

56-58, p. 31 (words not attributed to Christ):

This point has been dealt with above in # 49.

59, p. 31 (answers the claims of the liberal authors of the new Canon):

The fact that the liberals are either intellectually inept or dishonest in their error-filled defense of the N.O.M. has no bearing at all on whether or not the actual words of the new form fail to signify the same thing as the words of the traditional form; and that is the real issue.

67-69, p. 32 (Mass confers efficacy of Christ's Passion to Elect):

It is true that the efficacy of Christ's Passion is not communicated to all men, and that the Mass is the efficacious application of Christ's merits. However, Mr. Omlor is in error in his next point by failing to make proper distinctions. Christ's Passion is effective on a number of different levels: 1) conversions are a result of an effective application of the merits of Christ's Passion, even if the converted does not persevere, otherwise no conversion would have resulted at all; 2) justification is a result of an effective application of the merits of Christ's Passion, even if the justified one does not persevere, other wise no one could be justified; 3) salvation, of course, is the result of the full efficacy of Christ's Passion upon individuals.

70-71, p. 32 ("unto" and the sense of efficacy):

He says that "unto" means *to, towards,* or *leading up to,* thus "unto" conveys the sense of effectiveness. This is not entirely correct in terms of its common usage. That is, the word "unto" does not *necessarily* convey a sense of effectiveness; for I may be walking towards my home, but this does not mean that I will end up there. Passing a football *to* a wide receiver does not mean that it will get there. It is only when supplying a Catholic understanding to the word "unto" does it take on the meaning which Mr. Omlor here states. But then, this only supports my defense (Point II above), and refutes his position (Point III above). Once again,

Omlor lacks necessity to prove his point. Mr. Omlor appears to be looking for anything to argue against the new form, whether there is a basis or not.

72-77, p. 33 ("for many" vs. "for all;" efficacy vs sufficiency):

Besides being addressed and answered throughout this work, this particular section has been answered in my answers to objections VIII-IX from Point II.

78, p. 33-34 (makes point that the effects of the Passion are only upon those united to it):

Correct as stated, but has not yet proved that "for all" necessarily means all men both inside and outside the Church rather than "all" of the Elect, or "all" members of the Mystical Body. Mr. Omlor is still presenting points and arguments without yet proving that "for all" positively means something other than all members of the Mystical Body, even though his points and arguments depend *entirely* on this being so. How can any of his readers –who comprehend the content- not see this failure on his part?

79, p. 34 (No prayers for those outside Church, thus no prayers for all men):

Again, he has yet to prove that "for all" necessitates meaning others outside the Mystical Body. Nor has he yet proven that "for all" *cannot at all* mean "for all men within the Mystical Body," or "for all of the Elect." His point depends upon proof of this, but has yet to provide it. What we have here so far is the sowing of doubts in the minds of his readers without yet proving his foundational position concerning "for all."

80, p. 34 (New form denotes only sense of sufficiency):

The last sentence in section # 80 is simply an unsubstantiated conclusion. He never proves that the new form denotes only a sense of sufficiency, and this conclusion depends on his erroneous presumption that "for all" can *only* mean something other than "all" members of the

Mystical Body, or "all" the Elect. Once again, we have his conclusion before he has proven his starting point concerning "for all." However, it has already been proven in this work that "for all" can mean precisely this when understood "*according to the ancient and continual faith of the Universal Church*," as the Church demands of us (Point II above).

81, p. 34 ("may" denotes only possibility):

No, his conclusion does not follow. The use of "may" is valid for the reason that not ALL of the Elect have yet had all of their (ours, hopefully!) sins remitted. (There are probably some not born yet, others have not converted to the true Church yet.)

(See ADDENDUM at the end for refutations of some objections offered in regards to the word "may" used in the new form.)

82, p. 34 (Claims "for all men" cannot denote anything but sufficiency):

This is another unsubstantiated declaration and premature conclusion. Mr. Omlor erroneously presumes that "for all (men)" has only the meaning of universality. But we have proven to the contrary. As pointed out in **Point III**, he erroneously presumes that:

1. That "for all" necessarily means that which is contrary to proper signification and Catholic teaching (i.e. that it necessarily means all men of all time); and,

2. That "for all" can in no way signify that which is in accord with Catholic Teaching (i.e. it cannot be understood to mean "for all upon whom the shed blood of Christ is efficacious).

He has proven nothing, for it now appears that Mr. Omlor presumes by this point in his work that he has proven his case concerning what "for all" necessarily means (and what it cannot mean/signify). But, he has not. (See Points I - III above)

 # 83, p. 34 ("all men" and "unto" = heresy):

No, this also is not necessarily so, for supplied Catholic understanding (Point II above) refutes Mr. Omlor's conclusion (see also # 71 above).

 # 85, p. 34 ("for all" and sufficiency vs. efficacy):

Has yet to prove or demonstrate in any way this conclusion, for he has failed (not even tried) to prove that "for all' necessarily denotes sufficiency, and necessarily cannot denote efficacy "for all" the faithful members of Christ Mystical Body.(Point III above).

 # 87-109, pp. 35-38 ("Reality" of Sacrament is union of the Mystical Body):

This is simply a summary presentation of "the Reality" of the Sacrament and the relationship between the Holy Eucharist and the Mystical Body. We demonstrated how "for all" does signify the reality properly in Points I and III.

 # 110-111, p. 38 (Does "for all [men]" denote universal membership in Church?):

Amazing! Mr. Omlor is again guilty of a slight-of-hand here. This time, it is a different and more substantial one. He phrased the question in a misleading, and thus wrong, way. As mentioned before, the question is NOT, as Mr. Omlor states, to "ascertain whether ALL MEN can be considered members of the Body of Christ" (for we know this is not so), but whether or not the WORDS "for all (men)" of the new sacramental form necessarily imply or convey a universally inclusive meaning/sense of all men of all time belonging to the Body of Christ. We have proven that they do not (Points I and II above), and the lack of necessity works against his position (Point III above). We have proven that: 1) the words "for all" (and even "for all men") do not necessitate the meaning Mr. Omlor continually presumes they mean; and, 2) that when supplied with a Catholic understanding they mean precisely all members of the Mystical Body of Christ. Thus, it is indirectly proven that Mr. Omlor cannot prove his position without changing the very question. Shame on Mr. Omlor for changing THE fundamental question of the entire issue and misleading his readers.

118, p. 39 (All men and the Body of Christ):

He did it again! Though the conclusion is true in and of itself (i.e. that "all men" cannot belong to the Mystical Body of Christ), Mr. Omlor has phased it in a misleading (and self-serving) way. This entire issue is not whether the concept of all men -whereby its meaning is the universally inclusive sense - belong to the Mystical Body, but rather, whether or not the *words* "for all" in the sacramental form necessitate the universally inclusive meaning; and we know they do not. Mr. Omlor again deceives his readers and shifts their focus and attention to something other than the real matter at hand. He refuses to obey the dictates of the Church which declared at Vatican I that what she puts forth is "to be believed and held by all the faithful according to the ancient and continual faith of the Universal Church" (Pastor Aeternus). Thus we are required to understand the clause "for all (men)" as meaning for upon whom the Blood of Christ is efficacious.

120, p. 39 (new form "attacks" the *reality* of Sacrament):

His point here depends entirely upon having necessity of meaning, i.e., that all men of all time is the reference but, as demonstrated, such a meaning is not necessitated (Point III above). Thus, his conclusion cannot stand.

121, p. 39 (the Sacrament not "for all men"):

Same points of refutation found in numbers 110-111 and 118 above apply here.

125, p. 40 (different words = different Gospel):

He is still doing what he has done in numbers 110, 111, 118, 121: misleading by changing the question. However, this time he is simply buttressing his shifted notion, which we all agree upon (i.e. all men do not and will not belong to the Mystical Body of Christ), but that is not the issue as already pointed out.

126-27, p. 40-41 (Signification):

Mr. Omlor presumes that Pope Leo XIII's point in *Apostolicae Curae* (1896), whereby he states that the sacraments must signify the grace which they cause and that this signification is found chiefly in the form, works against the new form, but it does not. Mr. Omlor has yet to prove that the words of the new form in fact fail to signify the grace which they cause, whereas this author has proven they do not fail to signify what is proper to the Sacrament (Point II above).

130-131, p. 41 (Applying *Apostolicae Curae* to new form):

This point made by Pope Leo XIII can be used against Mr. Omlor and his position. Here's how: the words "for many" do not necessarily signify "ALL" the members of the Mystical Body, for they could (wrongly) be understood to mean simply "many of the Body of Christ" (but not all) or simply "many of the Elect" (but not all), and this would be a heretical sense. Therefore a Catholic understanding *must* be supplied to the traditional form. (See Answer to Objection VII, Point II above.)

136-137, p. 42 (short form fails to signify Mystical Body):

Though not material to the topic, it should be pointed out that Mr. Omlor's poor logic is affecting his theology. Here he leaves the reader with the impression that since Christ is not the Mystical Body, but only the Head of the Mystical Body, that therefore the Mystical Body is not Christ. Of course, he does not say this, but his argument implies this. So we ask: Is Christ the Head of a body which is something other than *His own Body*, or something other than *His own self?* No, of course not. Thus, his conclusion does not follow. As Pope Pius XII declared in *Mystici Corporis* (1943): "The Divine Redeemer together with His social Body constitutes one mystical person, the whole Christ... The Mystical Head, which Christ is, and the Church, His Mystical Body, which here on earth is as it were another Christ and takes His place, constitute the one new man... namely, Christ, head and Body; the whole Christ."

 # 139a, p. 42 (the form in St. Luke's Gospel):

According to Mr. Omlor's arguments this necessarily implies that the Mass offered by Christ according to St. Luke was invalid. Either that, or Christ offered the first Holy Mass according to a different rite, or a rite unique unto the God-man itself.

 # 141-142, p. 42 (new form signifies falsely):

Mr. Omlor is wrong. His conclusion erroneously presumes that "for all (men)" *necessarily* signifies the universally inclusive sense and that "for all" *necessarily* precludes the sense of all within the Mystical Body, or all for whom the blood of Christ is efficacious. But he has yet to prove his point, let alone disprove mine. His opinion (#'s 135-140) also erroneously presumes that "for all" cannot be understood in a proper Catholic sense. We have proven it can, therefore it must.

#'s 143-157, pp. 43-45 (different Sacramental forms):

Here he offers nothing against what this present author has presented as support of "for all" as signifying "all" the members of the Mystical Body, or "all" upon whom the Precious Blood of Christ is effective. But an important point is his acknowledgment that identical wording is NOT required for validity and the confecting of the Sacrament.

 # 160-161, pp. 45-46 ("for all" does not signify Mystical Body):

We have seen no such thing. Though arguing against the minimalists here, Mr. Omlor again erroneously presumes that "for all" cannot mean or signify all the members of Christ's Mystical Body, thus implicitly denying the principle and necessity of supplying a Catholic understanding. (Point II above).

 # 167-168, p. 47 (expounds upon the necessity of the long form):

Yes, this is true, but the form Omlor uses is required only for the traditional Latin/Roman Rite, this does not apply to the new rite of Paul VI. Mr. Omlor never deals with this point.

 # 175, p. 48 (new form fails to signify the *reality* of Sacrament):

Well, Mr. Omlor thinks has done it. He now pronounces his position/conclusion as if he has already proven that the new form with "for all…" is "foreign to and in conflict with the true meaning of the reality of

this sacrament, which is the union of the Mystical Body." But he HAS YET TO PROVE IT! He claimed back in # 35, p. 28 that he would show that "for all…" involves an *essential change in meaning*," but he never has. We have proven the contrary in Points I-III. (See also # 82 above.)

 # 178, p. 49 (changing the Consecration form):

Yes, grave sin is involved if additions or omissions are involved in pronouncing the forms *particular to each rite*. The N.O.M. is a different rite from the traditional Latin/Roman Rite, so this point does not apply and is a mute point from which to argue.

 # 191-92, p. 51 (new form not yet canonized?):

Amazing, he is still arguing, nay, concluding, as if he has already proven his point concerning "for all…" But he has not! This point, in #191, can only be true IF his arguments against "for all" had necessity on their side. But they do not. The new form does not necessitate that which is contrary to Catholic theology of the Mass.

 # 201-202, p. 52 (doubt concerning the new form):

This is also misleading, for the issue of doubt has not even been proven.

APPENDIX 2, pp. 56-60 (the use of certain words):

None of these examples address the REAL issue concerning "for all…" Besides, simply because some words/phrases can convey one notion does not mean that such a meaning is in fact necessitated. (See refutation of #'s 130-131, and also the sub-heading: APPLYING THE PRINCIPLE OF SUPPLIED UNDERSTANDING IN THE TRADITIONAL LITURGY in Point II above.)

APPENDIX 3, Objections A-C/ Replies, pp. 60-65 (St. Thomas and the Catechism of Trent):

Same point as above, and also, the principle by which Mr. Omlor argues here is the exact same one as what I have used concerning "for all;" that it does not necessarily mean that which is contrary to the Catholic teaching on the Mass. Thus, we have an inconsistency involved in Mr. Omlor's argumentation here. Also, this argument of Omlor's in using these sources has been answered above in the subsection entitled, "Authoritative Statements," Answers to Objection VIII (Point II above).

Reply to Objection E, last paragraph on page 66 ("for all" cannot denote properly):

Mr. Omlor is wrong in his argumentation here. The phrase "for all (men)" can denote "the elect only" by supplying a catholic understand to these words as we must to the words "for many" and numerous other phrases within each and every traditional rite. (Points I & II above)

Appendix 5, p.70 (Decree of Florence):

This is answered in my Point IV, # 3.

Epilogue, pp. 79 (conclusions concerning "for all" and new form):

-Third Paragraph: Mr. Omlor never proved in Part 12 of his work that the new form in fact suppresses what is essential and signifies falsely. He simply states that it does, expects his readers to see that it is "obvious" after all the doubts he has sown, and then builds the rest of his case around an unproven assertion. We have proven that he has no argument to stand on.

-Fourth Paragraph: This point, that the new form with "for all" fails to signify the *reality* of the Sacrament ,was never proven either. In fact, this argument of Mr. Omlor here is based on his slight-of-hand deception by changing the real question (see refutations of #'s 49, 110-111 above). We have proven in our Points I and III that the new form does properly signify the "reality" of the Sacrament.

"Has The Church The Right?"(pp. 82-90)

Does new form necessarily "violate those things which pertain to the integrity and necessary parts of the sacrament," as Mr. Omlor declares? Does the substitution of the words "for all" in place of "for many" constitute a " forbidden violation of the substance of the sacrament"? The answer is clearly NO, as proven in my first three points from above. Besides, Mr. Omlor never proves that the new form in fact does such violence. The arguments of this article are all answered in my four points above.

P. 85 (bottom): This is answered at the beginning of Point I above, as well as in my answers to objections IV and VI.

P.87, Interim Summary: These points all presume that the N.O.M. is not a new rite distinct from the traditional Latin/Roman Rite. (See my refutation of #'s 21-30, 168 and 178; see Point IV above under "Leonine Principle" near end of my # 1. See also, "A New Rite or the Revision of an Old Rite?")

The fact is, Mr. Omlor does not even address the REAL facts and arguments that exist against his position and which I have offered and expounded upon above. His conclusion is simply an avoidance of the truth.

Insights Into Heresy (pp. 91- 105)

Again, as with the above article, the arguments of this article against the validity of the N.O.M. are all answered and refuted in my Points I-IV above.

11: "For All Men Subverts Tradition"

P. 101 (first paragraph): This is a factual error fatal to Mr. Omlor's entire position. Though the exact three words "for all men" was never used before in the consecration, it has been proven that the words "for all" have been used before in approved rites. (See Point I above) Thus, his second question and answer in the fourth paragraph is based upon factual error.

12: "For All Men Subverts Sacramental Theology…" Pp. 102-03:

This point has been answered in the subsection entitled, "Authoritative Statements," Answers to Objection VIII (Point II above) as well as in my Point III above. But it must again be pointed out that everyone one of Mr. Omlor's articles following "Questioning the Validity" erroneously presume that he has already proven that "for all" necessarily changes signification and contradicts Catholic teaching on the Mass. Since he never has, and cannot, each and every subsequent argument and point that depends on this presumption is itself null and invalid.

RES SACRAMENTI (pp. 117-131)

The *Res Sacramenti* of the Holy Eucharist is the union of individual faithful with the Mystical Body of Christ. At the Council of Florence (1439), Pope Eugene IV, speaking of the traditional sacramental form, declared in *Exultate Deo* (On the Eucharist), "Finally, this is a fitting way to signify the effect of this sacrament, that is, the union of the Christian people with Christ" (Denz.698).

The fact is well made that the determining principle denotes the purpose or end for which the matter (bread and wine) is used. Thus a specific form of words is necessary for determining the end-purpose of the matter. The traditional form is "a fitting way to signify the effect of the sacrament" as Pope Eugene declared. But to say that one thing (or form) is fitting, is not at all to saying nothing else is fitting. We know that other forms are indeed fitting because the numerous other rites within the Church employ varying and different sacramental forms. Thus, it has been incumbent upon Mr. Omlor all along to prove that "for all" necessarily signifies something other than the traditional form, and he must prove that "for all" cannot determine the purpose of the matter (i.e. that it is not "fitting"). He has done neither. Again, we can't over-state the fact that Mr. Omlor has never demonstrated with any proofs that "for all" necessarily:

A. signifies the universally inclusive meaning; or

B. that the new form precludes the sense of "all" of the Elect, or "all" within the Mystical Body.

It has been proven in this work that such a necessity cannot be proven or exist (Point IV).

P. 126 (first paragraph): This only demonstrates that the word "many" is fitting. It is not at all an argument that "for all" cannot be used. (The rest of page 126 does not apply to this critique and defense since, as I made clear in my introduction, for the sake of argument on this point, we will argue with Omlor in his own court and presume that the short form is not sufficient.)

Pp. 127 (last paragraph)-128:

Mr. Omlor states: "It is OUR BELIEF that this vital signification (i.e., the unity of the Mystical Body) is found in the words of the form: "for you and for MANY." Three comments here:

- First, he presents this as only an opinion ("our belief"), not as a proven fact (i.e. it is Church teaching). Thus, he cannot bind men to his opinions.

- Second, and more importantly, what he says is true, but this does not mean that the vital signification is found ONLY in those words. It does not mean that because this vital signification is found in the words "for many" that it cannot be found in any other words. This would be illogical. It is like saying that I believe that revealed truths of God are found in the Bible. Okay, this is true, but the revealed truths of God are found not ONLY in the Bible, but also in Sacred Tradition. The fact that the vital signification is found in "for many' does not necessarily preclude that it can be found in "for all."

-Third, the words "for you and for many" are fitting for proper signification only when understood in light of Catholic teaching, and this very same principle (and requirement) also applies to the new form. Mr. Omlor is still working on his unproven (and, in fact, erroneous) presumption that "for all" necessarily signifies that which is contrary to Catholic teaching on the Mass, AND that it somehow cannot, nor does not, signify "ALL" the members of the Mystical Body. But we have proven that with the Catholic principle of supplied understanding the new form can and DOES signify such (see Point III above). Therefore, the form "for all" does indeed denote the purpose or end for which the matter (bread and wine) is used (union of ALL the faithful with the Mystical Body). Thus, it does provide proper signification and is not a "denial of the Mystical Body," as Mr. Omlor claims. (He also, as just mentioned, has logic working against him with this presumption -see Point IV.)

Pp. 128 (bottom)-129 (change in punctuation nullifies...):

This has to be one of the weakest arguments I have ever seen. This argument presumes that written punctuation can nullify an act of God. This argument is a classic example displaying the stubborn legalism of the Pharisees. It really is the result of a lack of supernatural faith. Who can believe that the power and action of Christ working through His priest can be nullified by a written punctuation mark (especially since the priest does not pronounce such marks)? No REAL Catholic believes such nonsense. Mr. Omlor must think God is more of a wimp than liberals think if the Almighty suddenly cannot (will not) do something based on different punctuation. The Priest only needs to intend what it is the Church does with this act, despite poor punctuation.

Under "Change of Meaning" (middle of p.129) Mr. Omlor says: "But no one can deny that there is in this new form an inherent change of sense or meaning." That's IT? This is his proof? This is no argument, nor any proof. It is simply his way of attempting to lead the reader into agreeing with his pre-concluded (and unproven) position concerning the new form. Therefore, I DO deny that there is an *inherent* change in sense, because both logic and the Catholic principle of supplied understanding prove that no such change is inherent in the new form. Once again, Mr. Omlor has yet to prove that the new form necessitates a change in sense or meaning. Each new argument continues to be built upon this erroneous presumption, and therefore cannot stand.

P.129 (bottom)-130: What is Wrong with "For All Men":

Mr. Omlor has done his slight-of-hand trick once again (see my refutation of #'s110-111 from "Questioning the Validity" above) by bringing up what is called a "red herring." Mr. Omlor has actually changed the REAL question and has shifted the focus of the entire argument from whether or not the WORDS "for all" can signify the same to whether or not the actual numerical sum of all men belong to Christ's Mystical Body. This is so terribly deceptive that one must by now question the good will of Mr. Omlor. Any high school student taking logic could recognize this shift.

Again, his ENTIRE argument stands upon his erroneous assumption that the words "for all" necessarily:

•change the signification;
• cannot designate the Res Sacramenti;

But Mr. Omlor has never proven such. He has no argument and no logical nor theological foundation upon which to stand. Here is the situation Mr. Omlor finds himself in:

1. He has in fact failed to prove his case;

2. He has been refuted and proven wrong in both his starting premise and in his conclusions.

P. 154: "Five Flaws Found":

In the second paragraph under the subheading, "The Eastern Liturgies," Mr. Omlor admits that identical wording is not required, but that the forms "should always be conformed to the same definite type." This necessarily means that having the same signification is what is at stake here, thus by the fact that the new form is faithful to the same meaning and signification of the old form, as proven in Points II and III above, then no argument can be used against it.

P. 220, "Church Couldn't Have Approved":

In the first paragraph on page 220, Mr. Omlor quotes St. Pius X about how the Church has no right to change anything touching on the substance of the sacraments. The substance of a sacrament is understood as that which makes the sacrament what it is, and without which there would be no sacrament. After the quote he draws a conclusion as if St. Pius was making this same point. But Mr. Omlor's conclusion does not follow, for he incorrectly presumes in his conclusion that altering the words is equivalent to changing the substance of a sacrament. This is both untrue and a contradiction to his own argumentation wherein he admits identical wording is not necessary (see #'s 143-146 on page 43 of *The Robber Church*).

Though it is true that to alter the words within a specific rite is a grave sin, it does not mean that the substance is necessarily changed, and even Mr. Omlor admits this fact. However, Mr. Omlor's argument is untrue in the sense that because there are numerous variations of the sacramental form of the Holy Eucharist found within the different approved rites of the Church there is therefore no ONE strict sacramental form for validity. Just above (p.154, *The Robber Church*) we saw that he admits that identical wording is not required so long as they conform to the same definite type.

Second Paragraph:

Though it is true that the Church has no power over the substance of the sacraments, Mr. Omlor still has not proven that the new form in fact involves a change in the essential form (i.e., signification). I have proven that it does not (Points II and III above).

Fourth Paragraph:

As a result of the above point, Mr. Omlor's "therefore" does not follow from what has preceded, thus his conclusion has no basis and is just plain wrong.

Fifth Paragraph:

His "consequently" does not follow as a result of his failure to prove that the new form *necessarily* changes signification.

"Questioning the Validity of McCarthy's Case"

Page 234-240:

Mr. Omlor continues to base his arguments and points upon his erroneous presupposition (disproved in my Point II above), for it has been proven in my Points I, II, & III that "for all" can and does convey a sense of efficacy faithful to Catholic teaching: i.e., for all upon whom the Blood of Christ is efficacious (or for all of the Elect).

Page 240, "Unto" Point on bottom half:

He defends "unto" despite the fact that it has other meanings which he even admits (see his footnote # 13 from this section in "Robber Church"). Therefore, "necessary signification" of words alone is not sufficient, but rather the supplied Catholic understanding provides proper signification. This is no different than what is required for the words "for all." Here we have a self-contradiction within the structure of Mr. Omlor's arguments. He applies the principle of supplied Catholic understanding in his arguments for "unto," yet he allows no consideration to the words of the new form.

Page 241-242:

This argument actually works against Mr. Omlor's, for by the very fact that he has to explain to us what the words of the traditional form mean and to what they refer. This fact therefore:

A. proves that clarity is not necessarily on the side of the traditional form without supplied Catholic understanding (and I have proven this in Point II above in Answer to Objection VII); and,

B. works against the criticism that because we must explain "for all" that it thus changes signification.

In other words, Mr. Omlor is *de facto* employing the principle of supplied understanding here while implicitly denying that it can (or should) be employed for the new form. This is both inconsistent and hypocritical. It is also self-defeating for him.

Page 243-244, Ambiguity in Sacramental Forms:

Once again, Mr. Omlor simply presumes what he has yet to prove (and cannot prove). The words "for all" do not *necessitate* ANY of these meanings. And, as proven above (Points II & III), a supplied Catholic understanding MUST be employed for numerous words (including "for many") from traditional rites. Thus, his conclusion that a sacramental form that is ambiguous is ipso facto invalid and therefore the new form is invalid cannot be substantiated, and thus not maintained. This is so by the very fact that when supplying the Catholic understanding to the new form, *as must be done for the old form*, the words are not at all ambiguous. The new form does not have multiple meanings when a Catholic understanding is supplied, just like "for many," when supplied with a Catholic understanding, does not mean for many of the Mystical Body, or for many of the Elect. His argument here is also invalid because he never takes into consideration this fact of the necessity of supplied Catholic understanding.

(The facts pointed out here, and in Points I-III above, also disprove the ICEL liberals arguments that the new form can mean more than one thing, and Omlor was arguing against them on this, with which I agree.)

Page 246, Fifth full paragraph:

Mr. Omlor is still doing what he is guilty of in #'s 110, 111, 118, 121 from QTV, that is, misleading by changing the question. The question is NOT whether ALL MEN in fact can be considered members of the Body of Christ (for we know this is not so), but whether or not the WORDS "for all (men)" of the new form necessarily convey a universally inclusive meaning/sense of all men belonging to the Body of Christ. We have proven that they do not (Points I and II above), and the lack of necessity in his arguments also works against his position (Point III above). Thus, his conclusion is based on what in logic is called a "red herring."

Page 247:

Under his, "My reply to this was as follows," Mr. Omlor begins his second paragraph with, "Secondly,…" This point has already been refuted and proven wrong in my critique of paragraphs 71-72, and 80-82 of QTV. I have proven that the new form does not convey both concepts of sufficiency and efficacy, but only the sense of efficacy -WHEN understood in light of Catholic teaching (i.e. Supplied Catholic Understanding, Point II above).

In the next paragraph, which begins with, "But, finally…," however, his conclusion is again wrong because it has been proven in Points II & III above that the phrase "for all (men)" can mean "the elect only" (i.e., ALL of the elect) and none others.

Pages 248-249, "If At First You Don't Succeed":

In the six points presented on these pages, Mr. Omlor:

1. fails to prove "for all" actually changes signification;
2. exposes his lack of faith in thinking that our Almighty Lord and His Divine action are nullified (and thus defeated) by a mere punctuation mark; (This author has never seen such a lack of faith in the Almighty before: His Sacred Action defeated by a mere punctuation mark!)
3. fails to recognize that the motivation of translators has nothing to do with actual meaning of words themselves, nor with what understanding the Church supplies for the words of approved sacramental forms;
4. fails in his attempts at right reasoning concerning the suppression of the words, "Mystery of Faith;" for such an omission does not necessitate an implicit denial of the dogma of the Real Presence. Again, the lack of necessity in his arguments render his points null;
5. brings up points which have no bearing on validity issue;
6. how they treat words has nothing to do with the words themselves. Mr. Omlor not only failed to succeed his first time, he failed again to prove his position.

No Mystery of Faith: No Mass?

In both articles, "The Necessary Signification in the Sacramental Form of the Holy Eucharist" (267-322) and "No Mystery of Faith: No Mass" (354-374), Mr. Omlor argues that since the words "mystery of faith" are not in the consecration formula of the N.O.M., that this also makes the N.O.M. invalid.

Before offering a few specific points of refutation, two points of general refutation are offered:

1. Mr. Omlor's position that this omission invalidates the N.O.M. is refuted by his own quotation from *De Defectibus* in # 20 (p. 358), whereby it is stated that the change MUST fail to signify the same as these words. But, as has been proven, the new form does not fail to signify the same sense. Thus, the lack of having the words, "Mystery of faith," does not invalidate the Mass.

2. The majority of the consecrations among the numerous rites of the Church do not have "the mystery of faith" (see the Appendix for examples). Thus, it is not essential and necessary for validity.

To say it is essential and necessary for the *traditional Roman/Latin Rite* is quite true, but this is to side step the fact that the *Novus Ordo Missae*, is just THAT, a NEW rite for the Western Church (see Point IV). The forms of one rite do not determine the forms of other rites. The N.O.M. is simply a new rite added to the Western Rite, which includes the Dominican Rite, Toledo Rite, Ambrosian (Milanese) Rite, Carthusian Rite, Anglican Use Rite, Sarumite Rite" (actually, The Sarum Use of the Latin/Roman Rite), as well as the Tridentine Rite.

These two general points alone refute this portion of Mr. Omlor's arguments. However, some additional points will be made to specific arguments and statements from these two articles.

P. 283-286, Section 8: What is Meant By "The Entire Form": **(expounds upon position that the entire form as necessary for validity)**

Mr. Omlor's point here buttresses my defense concerning the very fact that the exact form of the traditional Latin/Roman Rite is not essential to other rites. Mr. Omlor admits this both here and back on page 154, and this necessarily includes the new rite of Paul VI. So his arguments against the validity of the N.O.M. are obsolete and mute.

Pp. 303-306:

Mr. Omlor expounds upon and provides documents from both theologians and the Magisterium on the reality and effects of the Sacrament of the Holy Eucharist as "the union of the Mystical Body: that is, the strengthening of the recipient's bond of union with Christ, the Head of the Mystical Body, as well as with the other members." In the middle of this presentation, on page 304, he also criticizes some statements by Pope John Paul II. However, these are simply some personal opinions of the former Pontiff on the Holy Eucharist in general. Such statements do not mean that the N.O.M. is in fact such, or limited to such. Thus, there is no real argument against the N.O.M. here.

Pp. 311-13, # 11:

This argument by Mr. Omlor is about the "determining principle" found in the sacramental form. His denial that the new form signifies such properly is refuted in my "Answer to Objection VII", Point II (pp.25 ff), as well as in my refutation of #130-131 above (p.79).

P. 314 (2nd-3rd paragraphs):

Mr. Omlor simply asserts that the new form fails to signify (and even signifies falsely) the *Res Sacramente* (i.e. the union of the faithful with the Mystical Body of Christ). But he must prove that this is necessarily so, but he does not ever do such. We have proven that he cannot do such, and that the new form, as the Church uses and understands the words, does signify properly. Once again, Omlor simply asserts without any substantiation. His entire case rests on that which he never proves, but simply presumes. That which he presumes are the two points mentioned back at the top of page 41.

P. 325:

All of these points made by Mr. Omlor have been answered and refuted previously (see my Points I - III).

Pp. 326-327:

The addition of "the blood" does not subtly or otherwise succeed in destroying the four truths listed on page 327; for the use of this clause is an affirmation that in THAT chalice IS "the blood of the New and everlasting Covenant."

Pp. 368-369:

The quote used here by Mr. Omlor never says that the omission of "Mystery of Faith" invalidate the consecration, and *that* is the issue here. Besides, this document (a *Monitum* issued by the Holy Office on July 24, 1958) was dealing with and addressing those who said the traditional Latin/Roman Rite and thus omitted certain words. It was not dealing with any other rites, many which do not even include "mystery of faith." The N.O.M. of Pope Paul VI is a new rite. We also know that this clause is not necessary for validity since the numerous sacramental forms of other rites that omit it **do not**, in doing so, "omit what it ought essentially to signify" (Pope Leo XIII).

Pp. 370-374:

This entire section and argumentation still depends upon that which Mr. Omlor has never proven, as has been stated over and over again in this critique. This present work has proven that the new sacramental form does not touch upon or change in any way the substance of the Sacrament.

Mr. Omlor goes on to deny the authority of Pope Paul VI, or any pope, in establishing a new rite. However, one of the very Pontiff's Omlor invokes refutes his argument here. Pope Pius XII made clear in *Mediator Dei* (1947) that, while keeping the substance of the Mass and sacraments in tact (# 49), "the Sovereign Pontiff alone enjoys the right to recognize and establish any practice touching the worship of God, *to introduce and approve new rites, as also to modify those he judges to require modification*"(#58).

P. 372-373, # 92-93:

These points, that of accusing Pope Paul VI of touching (i.e. changing) the substance of the sacrament by omitting the words "mystery of faith" in the consecration, are not true since EVERY Vicar of Christ has allowed and approved over one dozen different rites with "*mysterium fidei*" being omitted. If Christ's Vicars have properly exercised their authority in allowing and approving such rites from the beginning, then when a particular Vicar of Christ introduces a new rite without it, he has neither invalidated the Mass, nor placed its validity in jeopardy, nor has he misused his Pontifical authority (though he may have lacked wisdom and prudence in doing so).

94-95 (pp. 372-373):

The four quotes referred to by Mr. Omlor (in # 94) ALL deal with the substance of the sacraments, yet it has already been demonstrated that the substance of the Sacrament of the Holy Eucharist has not been touched with the new form.

96 (p. 373):

This argument has no basis since the Roman Pontiff does have authority over ANY Monitum issued by the Holy Office, which is disciplinary in nature, as proven in my Point IV above. Besides, the *Monitum* was only in reference to those saying the traditional Latin/Roman Rite who might omit any words of the sacramental form, and thus it does not apply to the N.O.M. of Pope Paul VI or any other rite. Notice also, as pointed out above (Pp. 370-374 of Omlor), the *Monitum* does not say that omitting "*mysterium fidei*" invalidates the Mass, but that it is "nefarious" to do so, and is forbidden. Since the issue is validity, the use of this document is simply a distraction. Since the topic is about a new rite, the use of this document also is a distraction.

97:

It has already been proven that a Vicar of Christ, "by the mere stroke of a pen," can change anything he has authority over (see Point IV; see also second paragraph of my critique of pages 370-374 just above).

98:

This statement by Mr. Omlor, who accuses Pope Paul VI of defying Revelation by omitting "mystery of faith," is not at all applicable to Pope Paul VI and the N.O.M. Otherwise, EVERY Vicar of Christ is guilty of defying Divine Revelation for allowing and approving over one dozen rites which omit words spoken by Christ (i.e. "the mystery of Faith"). But this cannot be. Hence the error of Mr. Omlor's position and argument here.

#99:

Mr. Omlor accuses Pope Paul VI of being a liar in that he says when Paul VI as a priest, bishop and in his first few years as pope offered the traditional rite he admitted that our Lord said the words "mystery of faith" in the consecration of the wine (as Traditional tells us). But in offering the new rite of Mass Omlor asserts that Paul VI denied Our Lord stated these words. This conclusion and accusation against Pope Paul VI made by Mr. Omlor does not follow from the premise. For example, if one were to say that at the Sermon on the Mount, Our Lord stated, "Blessed are the poor in spirit, for theirs is the kingdom of heaven," he would be correct. *And in saying such, he would not be denying, even implicitly so, that Our Lord said more than that.* The same applies when a priest offers the N.O.M. Therefore, when Pope Paul VI omitted "the mystery of faith" from the new consecration form, knowing that Our Lord did speak these words, he nevertheless was not "tacitly admitting" that "he daily uttered a lie' when declaring in the traditional rite that Our Lord said these words.

The failure of Mr. Omlor to employ proper logic throughout his arguments has been fatal to his entire position. In # 104, page 373, he states: "In refuting me an *Adversarius* must first *disprove* (or attempt to do so) my case that Paul VI's *Novus Ordo Missae* is invalid"(italics in original). I have done so. Will he recognize his error? Only time will tell.

#100 ff:

As a result of the above critique and points of refutation made by this author, and also of Mr. Omlor's numerous failures, the sedevecantist and schismatic conclusions in numbers 100 forward therefore do not follow, but are invalid. He who set out to prove the invalidity of the all-English N.O.M. has only proven that his own position is what is invalid.

ADDENDUM

There has been a response to my refutation of #'s 70-72 (p. 74), and #81 (p. 76) above (p. 34 in *The Robber Church*), where Mr. Omlor states that "may" denotes only possibility, and thus cannot fulfill proper signification, since "may" implies "may not," and we know that this could never be applied to the Elect. The words "for all" in the new form, then, must be including more than the Elect, thus changing proper signification. What follows are those objections and my responses.

Objection: In order to buy the argument that "For all" is speaking of "all of the elect" you have to say that the words immediately proceeding "so that sins **may** be forgiven" can be speaking of the elect. But this is impossible. The word "may" necessitates that something **may not** happen. You cannot say that the elect may not have their sins remitted. Therefore the "for all" in the Novus Ordo cannot be referring to the elect but must be referring to some who may not have their sins remitted. This means that the "new form" is necessarily referring to sufficiency and not efficacy.

Answer: We must remember our context –that of a sacramental form. So the word is not employed simply in its secular/common usage, but in a technical sense -just like the words "for you and for many," and plenty of other terms, which take on a particular sacramental/theological meaning once employed within a sacramental formula, but do not necessitate such a meaning outside of such a sacramental context. (I demonstrate this substantially in Point II: The Principle of Supplied Catholic Understanding.) The word "may" in this sacramental formula does not necessitate that something (i.e., the forgiveness of sins) may not happen. Thus, his conclusion does not follow.

Objection: You cannot employ words which always connote a particular meaning in an unheard of way and then call it "technical". Miller is telling us that we have to understand "may" as meaning "towards" and leaving no possibility for "may not" even though may is never used in this way. This is false. This word "may" must necessarily leave open the possibility of "may not". Therefore it cannot be exclusively referring to the elect of which there is --no possibility that they "may not" (have their sins forgiven). You cannot use a word and then say that your meaning must be understood in an opposing way to it's usual signification to then salvage the orthodoxy of what would normally be understood as heretical.

Answer: According to the above objection, one cannot force a meaning/sense upon a word in which the word itself is never used and understood as such. This is true of itself, but this fact, this restriction does not apply to "may." Why not? We begin our answer to this with a question: Is their any precedence for the use of the word "may" that does not necessarily leave open the possibility of "may not," and thus can mean "shall," as in it SHALL occur? Yes. I know of two instances:

1. Prayers for the faithful departed, and

2. Legal usage in contractual law.

1. When Catholics pray for the dead, we only (and can only) pray for those souls detained in Purgatory; and the souls there WILL be going to Heaven. There is no chance for them not making it to the Beatific Vision. There is no possibility of them not eventually "resting in peace." They are among the Elect. Yet in officially approved prayers with indulgences attached to them, the word "may" is used with no such possibility as "may not" occurring.

"MAY the souls of the faithful departed rest in peace. Amen."

Here is a legitimate use of the word "may" applied to the Elect in reference to their Eternal End that does not in any way imply that this End "may not" be attained by them. In other words, there is no possibility -as to final outcome- that it "may not" happen for them.

2. In legal usage, along with its common usage as meaning permission, "may" also is used and understood as SHALL or MUST, particularly in contractual law; *"may" is used in such a way "where the sense, purpose, or policy requires this interpretation."* (Merriam-Webster Online Dictionary) See also *Black's Legal Dictionary*, under "Contractual Law" (the use of "may"), for the primary legal source.

Therefore, there is a "technical" usage of the word that is valid and employed that does not necessitate the possibility of "may not," but goes beyond the permissive sense, and means "shall." Even regular dictionaries recognize this usage (see fifth usage in The New International Webster's Concise Dictionary: "**may**... 5 Law Obligation or duty: *the equivalent of must or shall.*")

It should be made clear that we are never permitted to interpret the terms within an approved sacramental form in any way other than how the Church uses them (otherwise, this makes us no different than how Liberals and Modernists interpret both dogmatic formulas as well as sacramental forms). Since the word "may" does have a legitimate usage where "may not" is not necessarily implied, but has a more definite force as "shall," then the above accusation saying that the new form "employs words which always connote a particular meaning in an unheard of way" is unfounded, because it is factually incorrect.

Point VI

Was the New Mass Legally-Canonically Promulgated?

Some questions which will be dealt with in this section are: Was the New Mass of Pope Paul VI legally and properly promulgated? Is it a licit rite of the Holy Sacrifice of the Mass? Is it a mortal sin to attend the Novus Ordo Missae?

We shall deal with the latter question first. Is it a mortal sin to attend the Novus Ordo Missae? No. And no one has a right to say such. The N.O. Mass is a rite properly approved and promulgated by the Church. As problematic as it is, it cannot be a mortal sin to attend it, for it is a rite/ceremony promulgated by the Church. At the Council of Trent (Canon 7; "Holy Sacrifice of the Mass") it was declared:

> "If anyone says that the ceremonies, vestments, and outward signs, which the Catholic Church uses in the celebration of Masses, are incentives to impiety rather than the services of piety: let him be anathema."

The Church does not promulgate that which is intrinsically evil. As the Novus Ordo Mass (N.O.M.) was promulgated and is used by the Church, it cannot then be intrinsically evil. Therefore we cannot say it is a mortal sin to attend. However, as I demonstrated in Point IV under "Papal authority," the only way to get around this canon is to say that the Catholic Church did not promulgate this new rite, and thus does not use it (i.e. the Church is not present when this rite is performed), that would mean at least three things:

1. Any priest who offers the Holy Sacrifice with the new rite does so separated from union with the Church: (otherwise the Church IS there using this Rite and thus canon 7 is in effect);

2. Since Pope Benedict XVI (and Pope John Paul II befoe him) does offer the Holy Mass in this Rite, he is therefore separated from the Church and can not the visible head of the Church; and

3. that Pope Paul VI, who promulgated the new rite, was not a real pope.

Therefore, the only way around this canon, as applied to the N.O.M., is to hold that the chair of Peter has been vacant since before Pope Paul VI was elected. In other words, the only way to avoid the canonical condemnation of Canon 7 on the Mass is to be a sedevecantist, and be correct in that position (i.e. the Chair of Peter really has been vacant since before Paul VI, who promulgated the N.O.M.).

No one who acknowledges the legitimacy of the last four Roman Pontiffs can hold this position without being guilty of holding a position which is internally contradictory and thus refutes itself. One reason we know that the sedevecantist position cannot be sustained is that Pope Paul VI did properly and legally approve and promulgate the N.O.M., despite what some say about its legality.

LEGAL PROMULGATION

The the crux of this particular issue comes down to whether or not the New Mass of Pope Paul VI was legally and canonically promulgated. That is, what is the true status of the Liceity of the New Mass. Many who reject it hold that, even if it is essentially valid, it is illicit. They say it was not promulgated according to proper canonical norms. The "classic" argument put forth against the legality (or liceity) and proper promulgation of the *Novus Ordo Missae* is the following one by Father Francios Laisney of the S.S.P.X.:

> "the N.O. Mass was promulgated by Pope Paul VI with so many deficiencies, including the lack of proper juridical language to oblige all priests and faithful, that... there is no clear order, command, or precept imposing it on any priest." (*Angelus*, March, 1997)

Did Paul VI promulgate the N.O.M. without proper juridical language to oblige priests and the faithful? Did he fail to follow proper canonical norms? We will see that this accusation by Fr. Laisney is factually incorrect. Pope Paul VI did, in fact, properly and legally promulgate the new Mass. First, we must ask this question: What, in essence, is "promulgation"? To promulgate a law (or a norm) means nothing more than to announce it publicly by the lawgiver.

> "The essence of promulgation is the public proposal of a law to the community by the lawmaker himself, or on his authority, so that the will of the lawmaker to impose an obligation can become known to his subjects." ("Promulgation of Law," Washington, D.C., CUA Press, 1947)

The old 1917 Code of Canon Law, under which Pope Paul VI worked, simply says:

> "Laws enacted by the Holy See are promulgated BY THEIR PUBLICATION in the *Acta Apostolicae Sedis*, unless in particular cases another mode of promulgation is prescribed."(Canon 9)

This is all that the Code requires and it suffices to make known the WILL of the legislator, the Pope. Unless another provision has been made in a particular law itself, a law becomes effective (binding) three months after its official publication date in the Acta (Canon Law, # 9).

Now, on April 6, 1969, the Decree, "Ordine Missae" from the Congregation of Sacred Rites (Concilium) was promulgated by Paul VI's special mandate. This decree set 30 November, 1969, as the effective date for the legislation. Paul VI's Apostolic Constitution, "Missale Romanum" came out April 30, 1969. Though the Constitution of Paul VI was published in the "Acta," for some unknown reason the Decree was never published in the Acta. So Fr. Laisney and some other traditionalists hold that this omission means that the New Mass was never "duly-legally promulgated," and thus obliges no one.

But the argument over this slip is a red herring. Notice the second clause in canon 9: "unless in particular cases another mode of promulgation is prescribed." The key question in Canon Law about the promulgation of any law is the *will of the legislator*. So, it should be asked: Did Pope Paul VI manifest his will to impose on the faithful an obligation (i.e., the New Mass)? And did he do so in the Acta?

These questions are easily answered. In the April 30, 1969 "Acta Apostolicae Sedis" (AAS) we find the Apostolic Constitution "Missale Romanum" of Paul VI bearing his signature. Its heading states:

> "Apostolic Constitution. By which the *Roman Missal*, restored by decree of Vatican Ecumenical Council II, is PROMULGATED. Paul, Bishop, Servant of the Servants of God, for an everlasting memorial." (A.A.S. 61, 217-222)

The legislation, then, clearly meets the simple canonical norm for promulgation. The Supreme Legislator (i.e. the Roman Pontiff) needs no Decree from a cardinal for his law to "take." The New Mass is promulgated properly and the law is binding and normative. (This is precisely why the offering of and attendance at the Traditional Latin Mass is granted by an indult -but that is a separate issue.)

In the text of the Constitution, Pope Paul VI makes it abundantly clear that he is imposing the obligation of law on the faithful. For example:

1. The General Instruction preceding the New Order of Mass "IMPOSES NEW RULES for celebrating the Eucharistic sacrifice." (Latin of caps: *proponi, normae*)

2. "WE HAVE DECREED that three new Canons be added to this prayer [the Roman Canon]." (Latin of caps: *Statuimus*)

3. "WE HAVE ORDERED..." (Latin of caps: *jussimus*)

4. "All of which things WE HAVE PRESCRIBED by this, Our Constitution, shall begin to take effect from 30 November of this year." (Latin of caps: *praescripsimus*)

5. "IT IS OUR WILL that these laws and prescriptions be, and they shall be, firm and effective now and in the future." (Latin of caps: *volumus*)

We see that in our fifth example the supreme legislator understands himself as promulgating "laws and prescriptions" to be "firm and effective." Thus, despite what Fr. Laisney and others say, the standard Latin canonical and juridical terms a pope customarily employs to make a law are all present here:

- proponi, normae (# 1),
- statuta (# 2),
- jussimus (# 3),
- praescripta, (# 4),
- volumus (# 5)

Some of this is the very same language employed by Pope St. Pius V in *Quo Primum*. Both St. Pius V and Paul VI use identical lawmaking - canonical terms in key passages: "*norma*," "*statuimus*," and "*volumus*."

Some of the confusion on this entire issue on proper/obligatory promulgation was a result of a poor translation of example number 5 above. Poor translations of papal documents are part of the problem within the Church today. The first (and most popular) English translations of this passages read: "WE WISH that these prescriptions be effective..." So many concluded that Pope Paul VI was only wishing, and not obligating. The arguments were based upon this mistranslation. But the Latin word "*volumus*" is where we get the English, volition (i.e. to will, the faculty of the will, etc). Pope Paul was not merely wishing, he was expressing his will as supreme legislator that "*these laws and prescriptions be firm and effective now and in the future*." Can this be stated more clearly? (Even if it can, that's not to say that what we just read was not clear enough.) More significantly, in "*Quo Primum*," St. Pius V uses the exact same verb to impose the Tridentine Missal:

> "It is our will [L. *volumus*], however - and We decree by that same authority - that, after the publication of the Missal, and this Our Constitution, priests... be obliged to chant or read Mass according to this Missal."

In both cases, the Latin verb "*volumus*" expresses the essence of Church law-making: that is, the legislator's will to impose an obligation, or at least a norm, upon his subjects. Therefore, the will of the supreme legislator (i.e., the Roman Pontiff) was made clear, and has made clear that "*these laws and prescriptions be firm and effective now and in the future.*"

There are others who argue that no specific date was declared for obligation, and that this is necessary for proper/canonical legislation. Though the latter is true, the former is false. The Instruction "Constitutione Apostolica" was published in the AAS on 20 October, 1969. Therein it is clearly stated that by 28 November, 1971: "it shall become OBLIGATORY TO EMPLOY the [new] Order of Mass." The Instruction ends with this:

> "On 18 October, 1969 the Supreme Pontiff, Pope Paul VI, approved this Instruction, ORDERED IT TO BECOME PUBLIC LAW, so that it be faithfully observed by all those to whom it applies."

Therefore, those who hold and use the argument of no specific date are clearly in error.

+   +   +   +   +   +

It should be clear now, that the New Mass has been duly, and legally, and properly promulgated by the proper authority to do such: the Roman Pontiff. It has also been demonstrated that the new form of the N.O.M. does not involve an essential change in meaning in the sacramental form, and that it does NOT suppress what is essential, nor signify falsely what it ought, but is a valid form appropriate for this new rite of the Mass. Therefore, in accordance with Canon 7 from Trent quoted above, it cannot be a mortal sin on the part of the faithful to attend this Mass.

One final objection shall be answered concerning this matter. With all the confusion that exists, there is at least some legitimate doubt concerning the promulgation of the N.O.M. Dr. Coomaraswamy says in his book "The Problems with the New Mass," (p.63):

"Certainly in the face of the evidence given, they [conservatives] must, at the very least, agree the matter is open to debate. But if it is open to debate, there is doubt -and above all there is doubt with regard to the form of the Consecration."

We answer, certainly in the face of the evidence presented in this work, the matter is not open to debate. Thus, there can be no doubt in the objective realm. And simply because some individuals have personal doubts does not mean that doubt actually-objectively exists concerning the validity of the Mass. No one, layman or priest, has the moral right (let alone duty) to cause others to doubt because of his own subjective mental state of doubt. This is a principle of moral theology. Those who have doubts have such doubts based on ignorance and MISinformation, and this is not a basis for either doubting or for opening it up to debate.

The existing canonical legislation of the Church has legally and canonically promulgated a new rite of Mass. The faithful must accepted it as such. In fact, Pope Pius XII declared in *Mediator Dei*:

> Moreover, can no Catholic in his right senses repudiate existing legislation of the Church to revert to prescriptions based on the earliest sources of canon law.

What can be concluded is the following: if the Catholic Church pronounces that a particular sacramental rite is a sufficient and proper vehicle for conferring a particular sacrament, as mentioned before, then it is valid and the faithful must accept it as such. The Church has done so for the N.O.M., therefore we the faithful must accept it as valid and legally promulgated.

"We decree that these laws and prescriptions be firm and effective now and in the future, notwithstanding, to the extent necessary, the apostolic constitutions and ordinances issued by our predecessors and other prescriptions, even those deserving particular mention and amendment" (Pope Paul VI, *Missale Romanum*, 3 April 1969; AAS 61 [1969] 217-222).

APPENDIX I

Approved Variations in the Sacramental Form for the Consecration of the Wine

The Church has approved of numerous Consecration forms among the differing Catholic Eastern Rites, and in doing so has in no way touched upon, let alone changed, the substance of the Sacrament. I call your attention particularly to numbers five and six. (Taken from: "The Liturgies of St. Mark, St. James, St. Clement, St. Chrysostom and the Church of Malabar," 1859; by Father J. M. Neale)

1. THE ANAPHORA ACCORDING TO THE ORDER OF THE HOLY CATHOLIC AND ROMAN CHURCH , THE MOTHER OF ALL THE CHURCHES.

The wording is "FOR THIS IS THE CHALICE OF MY BLOOD, OF THE NEW AND ETERNAL TESTAMENT, THE MYSTERY OF FAITH: WHICH FOR YOU AND FOR MANY SHALL BE POURED FORTH FOR THE REMISSION OF SINS."

2. THE ANAPHORA OF ST. PETER, HEAD OF THE APOSTLES.

The wording is "THIS IS MY BODY, WHICH FOR YOU AND FOR MANY IS BROKEN AND IS GIVEN FOR THE EXPIATION OF CRIMES, THE REMISSION OF SINS, AND LIFE ETERNAL".

3. THE ANAPHORA OF THE TWELVE APOSTLES.

The wording is "FOR THIS IS THE NEW TESTAMENT IN MY BLOOD, WHICH FOR YOU AND FOR MANY IS POURED FORTH FOR THE EXPIATION OF SINS AND LIFE ETERNAL".

4. THE ANAPHORA OF ST. JAMES.

The wording is "THIS IS MY BLOOD OF THE NEW TESTAMENT, WHICH FOR YOU AND FOR MANY IS SHED AND DISTRIBUTED FOR THE REMISSION OF SINS".

5. THE ANAPHORA OF ST. JOHN THE APOSTLE AND EVANGELIST.

The wording is "THIS IS THE CHALICE OF MY BLOOD OF THE NEW TESTAMENT: TAKE, DRINK YE OF IT: THIS IS SHED FORTH FOR THE LIFE OF THE WORLD, FOR THE EXPIATION OF TRANSGRESSIONS, THE REMISSION OF SINS TO ALL THAT BELIEVE IN HIM FOR EVER AND EVER.

6. THE ANAPHORA OF ST. MARK THE EVANGELIST.

The wording is "THIS IS MY BLOOD OF THE NEW TESTAMENT; TAKE, DRINK YE ALL OF IT, FOR THE REMISSION OF SINS OF YOU AND OF ALL THE TRUE FAITHFUL, AND FOR ETERNAL LIFE".

7. THE ANAPHORA OF ST. XYSTUS, THE POPE OF ROME.

The wording is "FOR THIS IS THE CHALICE OF MY BLOOD OF THE NEW TESTAMENT, WHICH FOR YOU AND MANY IS GIVEN FOR THE EXPIATION OF CRIMES, AND HATH GIVEN TO US THE REMISSION OF ETERNAL LIFE".

8. THE ANAPHORA OF ST. JOHN CHRYSOSTOM.

The wording is "THIS IS MY BLOOD WHICH CONFIRMS THE TESTAMENT OF MY DEATH: WHICH FOR YOU IS POURED FORTH, AND FOR MANY IS GIVEN AND DIVIDED, TO THE PROPITIATION OF TRANSGRESSION, THE REMISSION OF SINS, AND LIFE ETERNAL".

9. THE ANAPHORA OF ST. BASIL.

The wording is "THIS IS THAT MY BLOOD. WHICH FOR YOU AND FOR MANY IS POURED FORTH AND SPRINKLED, FOR THE EXPIATION OF TRANSGRESSIONS, AND REMISSION OF SINS, AND FOR LIFE ETERNAL".

10. THE ANAPHORA OF ST. CYRIL.

The wording is "THIS IS MY BLOOD WHICH SEALS THE TESTAMENT OF MY DEATH, AND PREPARES YOU AND MANY OF THE FAITHFUL TO ETERNAL LIFE".

11. THE ANAPHORA OF ST. DIONYSIUS.

The wording is "THIS IS MY BLOOD OF THE NEW TESTAMENT, WHICH FOR YOU AND FOR MANY IS POURED FORTH AND GIVEN FOR THE EXPIATION OF TRANSGRESSIONS, THE REMISSION OF SINS, AND LIFE ETERNAL".

The form for some of the other rites are as follows:

For the Byzantine(Divine Liturgy of St. John Chrysostom):

The form is: "THIS IS MY BLOOD OF THE NEW TESTAMENT WHICH IS SHED FOR YOU AND FOR MANY FOR THE FORGIVENESS OF SINS".

For the Armenian:

The form is: "THIS IS MY BLOOD OF THE NEW TESTAMENT WHICH IS SHED FOR YOU AND FOR MANY FOR THE EXPIATION AND FORGIVENESS OF SINS".

For the Coptic:

The form is: "FOR THIS IS MY BLOOD OF THE NEW COVENANT, WHICH IS SHED FOR YOU AND FOR MANY FOR THE FORGIVENESS OF SINS".

For the Ethiopic:

The form is: "THIS IS MY BLOOD OF THE NEW COVENANT, WHICH SHALL BE POURED OUT AND OFFERED FOR THE FORGIVENESS OF SINS AND ETERNAL LIFE OF YOU AND MANY".

For the Chaldean:

The form is: "THIS IS MY BLOOD OF THE NEW COVENANT, THE MYSTERY OF FAITH, WHICH IS SHED FOR YOU AND FOR MANY FOR THE FORGIVENESS OF SINS".

For the Malabar:

The form is: "FOR THIS IS THE CHALICE OF MY BLOOD OF THE NEW AND ETERNAL TESTAMENT, THE MYSTERY OF FAITH, WHICH IS SHED FOR YOU AND FOR MANY FOR THE REMISSION OF SINS".

BIBLIOGRAPHY

Bouyer, Louis, Rev. *Eucharist,* Trans. C. H. Quinn, Notre Dame, IN, University of Notre Dame Press, 1968

Cekada, Anthony, Rev. *The Problems with the Prayers of the Modern Mass*, Rockford, IL, Tan Books and Publishers, Inc., 1991

Coomaraswamy, Rama P. *The Problems with the New Mass*, Rockford, IL, Tan Books and Publishers, Inc., 1990

Davies, Michael. *Pope Paul's New Mass*, Vol. Three: Liturgical Revolution, Kansas City, MO., Angelus Press, 1980

Davies, Michael. *The Eternal Sacrifice: The Liturgy Since Vatican II*, Long Prairie, MN., The Neumann Press, 1987

Denzinger, Henry, Rev., *The Sources of Catholic Dogma* ("Enchiridion Symbolorum"], 30th ed., trans. Fr. Roy Deferrari, 1954, Herder & Co., reprinted by Loreto Publications

Masure, Canon Eugene. *The Christian Sacrifice*, Trans. By Dom Illtyd Trethowan, London, Burns Oates & Washbourne LTD., 1944

Omlor, Patrick Henry. *The Robber Church: The Collected Writings, 1968-1997*, Ontario, Canada, Silvio Mattachione & Co., 1998

Ottaviani, Alfredo, Most Rev., Bacci, Antonio, Most Rev. *The Ottaviani Intervention: Short Critical Study of the New Order of Mass*, Trans. Rev. Anthony Cekada, Rockford, Il., Tan Books and Publishers, Inc., 1992

Pius V, Pope. *Quo Primum Tempore*, 1570, from *Missale Romanum*, Washington, D. C., National Catholic Welfare Conference, Inc., 1964

Roman Missal, NCCB, Washington, D.C., Benziger Brothers, 1964, 1970

Trinchard, Paul, Rev. *New Mass in Light of the Old*, Monrovia, CA., Marian Publications, Inc. 1995

Trinchard, Paul, Rev. *The Abbot & Me on Liturgy*, Metairie, LA., Maeta, 1997

Wathan, James F., Rev. The Great Sacrilege, Rockford, Il., Tan Books and Publishers, Inc., 1971

About the author:

Adam Miller is married and the father of eight children. He graduated *Summa cum laude* in his majors of theology and philosophy from Mount St. Mary's College (now University) in Emmitsburg, MD. With graduate work done in theology, he is a member of both *Phi Sigma Tau*, the national honor society in philosophy, and *Theta Alpha Kappa*, the national honor society in theology.

Mr. Miller has taught high school religion and catechism for twelve years, and is the founder and director of Tower of David Ministry and Publications, a lay Catholic educational apostolate. The author of more than one dozen works defending and explaining Catholic teaching and history, Mr. Miller is finishing up a text on American history from a traditional Catholic perspective.

Mr. Miller is available for talks at parishes, schools, seminars and conferences. He welcomes correspondence at:

11910 Wonder Ct.
Monrovia, MD 21770
or
E-mail: Tower_of_david@netscape.com

See Tower of David Ministry's web page at:
http://www.geocities.com/adam_todm/index.htm